Hello

Think of us as a blue plate special with a slice o' pie to boot. Meaty, dependable, and affordable for all. We thought to ourselves: take a big helping of thoughtful guidance and add a side of straightforward instruction and you'd have a start on a pretty good book. Offer it all for less than the price of a couple of movie tickets, and you'd have a great book. In fact, you've got that book in your hands.

Each book in this series of introductory guides isolates one application or topic and aims to get you exploring it quickly and effectively. They're action-based, non-comprehensive, and not filled with a lot of idle chat because our goal is to get users using. Our books are for those who do not accept the premise that if you don't already know, you must be a dummy or an idiot. We believe in using computers to DO things, not doing things to use computers. Your computer should make your life better, not more complicated. And the truth is, despite the ease of use offered by today's computers, users often need a bridge to help them navigate the digital world. They need a real-world guide and they need it with no nonsense.

You'll be surprised how far you can go in 200 or so pages. Take a look at the Table of Contents. Well, go ahead. See what we mean? Simple. Straightforward. *Load. Edit. Embellish.* That's the way using a computer should be. And that's the way each book in this series works. Inside each of these handy books are the essentials of each topic—everything you need to know to get up and running.

Thanks for picking up our books, and drop us a line with your comments.

Create!

the *no nonsense* guide to

Photoshop Elements 2

Greg Simsic
Katy Bodenmiller

McGraw-Hill/Osborne
New York Chicago San Francisco
Lisbon London Madrid Mexico City
Milan New Delhi San Juan
Seoul Singapore Sydney Toronto

The *McGraw·Hill* Companies

McGraw-Hill/Osborne
2600 Tenth Street
Berkeley, California 94710
U.S.A.

To arrange bulk purchase discounts for sales promotions, premiums, or fund-raisers, please contact **McGraw-Hill**/Osborne at the above address. For information on translations or book distributors outside the U.S.A., please see the International Contact Information page immediately following the index of this book.

Create! The No Nonsense Guide to Photoshop Elements 2

1234567890 DOC DOC 019876543

ISBN 0-07-222738-9

Publisher Brandon A. Nordin	**Indexer** Jack Lewis
Vice President & **Associate Publisher** Scott Rogers	**Computer Designers** Mickey Galicia, Jim Kussow, John Patrus, Dick Schwartz
Executive Acquisitions Editor Jane Brownlow	**Illustrators** Melinda Moore Lytle, Michael Mueller, Lyssa Wald
Project Editor Katie Conley	**Series Developers** Katy Bodenmiller, Greg Simsic
Acquisitions Coordinator Tana Allen	**Series Interior Design** Katy Bodenmiller, Greg Simsic
Technical Editor Rowena White	**Series Cover Design** Katy Bodenmiller, Greg Simsic
Copy Editor Peggy Gannon	**Cover Illustration** Hulton/Archive
Proofreader Susie Elkind	

This book was composed with Corel VENTURA™ Publisher.

About the Authors

Greg Simsic is an artist living and working in New York City who has penned four previous Photoshop books—all of which emphasize simple, clear direction, which some say are an antidote to his otherwise altogether aimless sojourns.

Katy Bodenmiller has used Adobe's digital-imaging products for over a decade and presently earns a living as a graphic designer with the help of current Adobe products.

Thanks

Scott, for the opportunity.

The entire OMH team—especially Jane, Margie, Tana, Dodie, Kate, Jenn, Elizabeth, and Dick—for their tireless support and patience.

Katie, Peggy, and Rowena, for making this a better book.

Jeff, for the encouragement, occasional scolding, and frequent red penning.

Kelli, for the expert advice.

Adobe, for a great product.

Contents

Chapter 1 Acquaint **1**

Start 2

   The Welcome Screen 2

      New, Browse, and Connect 2

      Common Issues and Tutorial 2

   Know the Work Area 3

Open an Image 4

   The Image Window 4

   The Status Bar 6

   Turn On Rulers 7

   Resize an Image Window 7

Choose Menu Commands 7

   View Windows 8

      Retrieve the Welcome Screen 8

   Change an Image 8

      Flip 8

      Rotate 8

   Take a Shortcut 9

Step Backward 9
Key Commands 9

Use Palettes 10
View a Palette 10
Combine Palettes 11
Dock Palettes 12

Wield Tools 13
Select a Tool 13
Selection Tools 13
Creation Tools 13
Retouch Tools 13
Miscellaneous Tools and Color 14
Set Tool Options 14

Change Your View 15
Magnify 15
Zoom Tool 15
Navigate the Image Area 16
Navigator Palette 16

Boost Performance 17
Set Preferences 17
Random Access Memory 17
Scratch Disks 18

Learn More 19
Hints 19
How To 19
Help 20

Chapter 2   **Get Images** **21**

Understand Images 22
Know What Kind 22
Bitmap Images 22
Vector Images 23
Change Size and Resolution 23
Resize 24
Resample 25
Go Back to the Drawing Board 26
Know Color Modes 27
RGB Mode 27
Indexed Color Mode 27

Grayscale Mode 28
Bitmap Mode 29
Change Canvas Size 29

Open Images 30
Open Recent Images 31
Open Other File Formats 32
EPS 32
PDF 33
Photo CD 33

Browse 34
The File Browser 34
Find a File 35
Customize the Browser 36
Rename Files 36
Organize Files 36

Connect to a Camera or Scanner 37
Import Photos 37
Import Scans 38
TWAIN 39
WIA 39
Video Stills 39

Chapter 3   **Retouch** **41**

Understand Color 42
The Plain Truth 42
Calibrate Your Monitor 42

Fix Quick 44
Quick Fix 45
A Scan 46

Balance Light and Dark 47
Compensate for Bad Lighting 47
Fill Flash 47
Adjust Backlighting 48
Improve Contrast 48
Levels 49

Correct Color 51
Remove a Color-Cast 51
Color-Cast Command 51
Color Variations 52

Improve Color Balance 53
  Auto Color Correct 53
Enhance Color 53
  Saturation 53
  Hue 54
  More Flexibility 54

Fix Flaws 56
  No More Red Eye 56
    Red Eye Brush 56
  Cover-Up 57
    Smudge 57
    Clone Tool 57

Fine-Tune 59
  Sharpen Details 59
    Unsharp Mask 59
    Pin-Point Sharpen 60
  Soften Harsh Edges 61
    Blur Tool 61

Chapter 4 **Select** **63**

Crop an Image 64
  Crop Tool 64
  Adjust the Crop 65

Make a Simple Selection 66

Make an Irregular Selection 67
  Set Lasso Options 68
    Selection Mode 68
    Anti-Alias 68
    Feather 69
  Use the Lasso 69

Add to a Selection 70

Subtract From a Selection 71

Copy and Paste 72

Flip, Scale, Rotate, and Move 73
  Flip 73
  Scale 73
  Rotate 74
  Move 74

Make a Complex Selection 75
   Set Options 76
      Selection Mode 76
      Feather and Anti-aliased 76
      Width, Edge Contrast, and Frequency 76
   Use the Magnetic Lasso 77

Modify a Selection 79
   Grow 79
   Similar 80
   Expand or Contract 80
   Smooth 80

Incorporate a Copy 81
   Make It Seamless 81
      Remove a Halo 81
   Make it Convincing 82
   Use the Magic Wand 82
      Select the Inverse 83

Chapter 5   **Add Type** **85**

Create Type 86
   Enter Type 86
   Edit 87
   Format 87
      Change the Font 88
      Resize 88
      Anti-Alias 88
      Align 89
      Pick a Color 90
      Change Orientation 90
      Move It 90

Warp 91
   Make Waves 91

Transform 93
   Skew 93
   Change Perspective 94

Add Depth 95
   Bevels 95
   Shadows 96
   Plastic 96

Fill Text 97
   Rusted Metal 97
   Easy Patterns 98
   Rusted Metal Revisited 98

Chapter 6   **Paint** **101**
Collect Materials 102
   Start a Blank Canvas 102
   Color Palette 103
      Foreground/Background 103
      Color Picker 103
      Swatches Palette 104
   Choose a Brush 107
      Select the Brush Tool 107
      Brushes Pop-Up Palette 107
   Erase 109

Paint to Canvas 110
   Fill With Paint 110
      Gradients 110
      Paint Bucket 111
   Customize a Brush 113
      Size 113
      Spacing 113
   Blend Colors 115
      Opacity and Fade 116
      Smudge 116

Mix Media 117
   Colorize an Image 117
   Turn a Photo Into a Painting 118
      Impressionist Brush 118

Chapter 7   **Combine Images** **121**
Build a Layered File 122
   Create a Background 122
   Add a Shape 123
      Change Color 124
      Simplify Layer 124
   Add Type 124

Understand Layers 125
    Layers Palette 125

Arrange Objects 128
    Move 128
    Reorder 129
    Link 130

Blend Images 130

Make an Image Transparent 131

Mask an Image 132
    Lock Transparency 132
    Group Layers 133

Add Image Layers 134
    Duplicate Layers 134
    Drag Layers 134

Clean It Up 135
    Lock 136
    Delete 136
    Merge 137
    Flatten 137
    Save As 138

Make a Panorama 138

Chapter 8   **Embellish** **143**

Be an Artist 144
    Filters 144
    Impressionist 145
    Surrealist 146

Create an Illusion 148
    Water 148
    Glass 148

Add Movement 149
    Blur 149
    Wind 149
    Double Vision 150

Set the Mood with Lighting 150
    Lens Flare 150
    Lighting Effects 151

Create Shadows and Glows 153
  Drop Shadows 153
  Glows 156

Frame a Photo 157
  Photo Corners 157
  Brushed Aluminum Frame 158
  A Frame of One's Own 159

Create Textures and Backgrounds 162
  Texturize 162
  Start with Color 162
  Clouds 164

Chapter 9   Present 167

Save Images 168
  Save 168
    First Save 168
    Name Your File 168
    File Format 169
    Choose a Destination 169
  Save As 170
    Change the File Format 170

Print 172
  Print Preview 173
    Page Setup 173
    Scale 174
  Resolution 174
  Paper 174

Save Paper 175
  Picture Package 175
  Contact Sheet 176

E-mail an Image 177

Present a Slide Show 178
  Select Images 178
  Direct Your Show 179
  View Your Slide Show 179

Prepare an Image for the Web 179
  Save for Web 180
  Use a Predefined Setting 181
  Fine-Tune the Settings 181

Image Size 181

Optimization Information 181

Create a Photo Gallery 182

Gather Images 182

Setup 183

Choose an Image Folder 183

Choose a Destination 183

Choose Options 184

Banner 184

Choose Image Size 184

Make Elements Work 185

Index **187**

Welcome

You've probably heard it all before: you're about to embark on a great adventure; this software will change your life, make it better; you'll wonder how you ever lived without the information in this book. While all of that's true for this book, we know the bottom line is you want to do stuff with Adobe Photoshop Elements 2. That's why we're here—to show you how to do stuff.

You want to revive old photos, draw a mustache on your sister's face, or maybe slap a dog's head on your brother's body. You want to save and organize and enlarge and print your own photographs. Or maybe you want to make your own digital paintings and web graphics. While we can't show you how to pull off every harebrained scheme you can dream up, we can teach you the fundamentals, point you in the right direction, and provide some practical advice along the way.

In the interest of getting to the heart of the matter, you'll find that the chapter titles tell you just what you'll learn to do. Take Chapter 6, for instance. It's titled "Paint," because that's what you'll do: you'll learn how to pick colors, use a paintbrush, and blend your brush strokes. We even give you a few pointers on how to compose a painting and use the paint tools in unexpected ways.

The book starts with a couple of chapters that ease you into Elements. A basic introduction to Elements is followed by tips on navigating the workspace, and a primer on image files and how to open them. But the heart of the book is the fun stuff that follows, from adjusting the colors and lighting in an image, to making an image look like an impressionist painting, to creating a painting from scratch. And if that's not enough, in the last chapter you'll learn how to publish all your hard work. If you want to e-mail an image to a friend, for instance, that's where you'll learn how to do it.

Any way you slice it, it'll be easy. Just follow our lead, take our advice, and remember to experiment and explore on your own. Above all, don't let Elements intimidate you. Sure, it's powerful and it can achieve some mind-bending results, but it's just a piece of software, a tool. You're the boss—and don't forget it.

Before you dive in, just to make sure we're on the same page, here are a few things about the conventions we've employed in this book:

Menu Commands   When you see bold words in series separated by vertical bars, this is a menu command. For example, when you see **File | Open**, it means that you first click **File** in the menu bar to reveal a menu of commands, then move the cursor to the **Open** command in the menu to select it and click the mouse again.

Keystrokes   Strings of bold words or letters in small caps that are joined by hyphens represent keystrokes or keystroke combinations. Normally, these instances are preceded by the verb "press." In the case of **CTRL-CLICK**, press and hold the **CTRL** key as you click the mouse button. If the keystroke combinations contain more than one or two keys, as in **SHIFT-OPTION-DELETE**, press and hold all but the last key. With the first keys engaged, press the final key to complete the command.

> ***AS A MATTER OF FACT***   *Text that appears in boxes like this one provides extra information about a topic. It may expand your knowledge of an issue, warn you of a potential problem, or provide a helpful workflow tip.*

All that said, it's time to get to the business of learning something about Adobe Photoshop Elements 2.

Acquaint

To be successful at anything, you've first got to learn the fundamentals. Say you want to make a soufflé. It'd be impossible to do it if you didn't know a whisk from a bowl or an oven from a fridge. In the same way, it would be mighty hard to use Elements if you weren't first equipped with a few basics. This book aims to get you using Elements as soon as possible. But we also want you to use it efficiently and effectively and that means spending a little time getting to know the What and Where. In the chapters that follow, you'll learn to tackle the How. Just think of this chapter as the primer on where to find stuff in the kitchen; and the rest of the chapters are the recipes and cooking classes.

While your kitchen may not be the model of efficiency and good order, you likely know where to find a spoon, spatula, or pan when you need one. For the system to work, you have to put stuff back where it belongs. The pan goes back to the pot rack, the spoon back in the drawer, and the spatula in the utensil holder by the stove. The same principle holds with the Elements Work Area. Everything is in its place. That's what we'll focus on in this chapter: where you'll find the tools of the image-editing trade and how you can expect to use them. And we might even throw in a few food safety tips to boot.

As with the other chapters in this book, our goal here is to give you some practical advice to point you in the right direction before sending you on your way. We can't cover every nook and cranny of every topic, however. Besides, most of us learn by doing. So use this chapter (and all others in the book) as a guide, then go experiment on your own.

Start

When you launch Elements, you've probably got one of three things in mind: creating an image from scratch, opening an existing one, or importing one from a scanner or digital camera. Elements, smart as it is, anticipates your needs and offers a quick way to start each of these tasks by allowing you to choose from several options presented in the Welcome Screen, which appears each time you launch the program. While it is convenient, you don't really *need* the Welcome Screen to get started; you can open or start images by other means. In our opinion, you're better off first understanding those other means. Once you do, the Welcome Screen's usefulness will make more sense. So let's take a quick look at the Welcome Screen and then move on to opening an image using a different method.

The Welcome Screen

If you haven't already, launch Elements by double-clicking its application icon in the Adobe Photoshop Elements 2 folder on your hard drive (if you don't know where this folder is located, choose Find from the Start menu [Windows] or from the File menu [Mac] and search to locate it). Once Elements launches, the Welcome Screen pops up to greet you: It's the big box with the sunflower image that you see in the middle of your screen. This is Elements way of saying "Hi" and telling you it's ready to start a work session. Now you just have to tell it what to do. The Welcome screen offers five options; each option is a specific way to start a work session in Elements (see Figure 1-1).

New, Browse, and Connect

The first three options in the Welcome Screen are grouped together because they are the most commonly used. New File tells Elements that you want to begin with a blank slate; Browse for File is used when you want to open an existing image or manage your image files; and the last of these three will interest you if you use a scanner or own a digital camera—Elements can connect directly to them with the Connect to Camera or Scanner option. (Browsing and importing images from these devices is discussed in Chapter 2.)

Common Issues and Tutorial

Your next two options are a little different. Unlike the first three, they aren't ways to open images in Elements. Instead, they are help resources. The Common Issues option shows you a menu from which you can choose to learn how to accomplish some simple and common tasks, while the Tutorial option provides you with step-by-step instruction for using a range of Elements' features. Be sure to check out both of these options before you move on to Chapter 2.

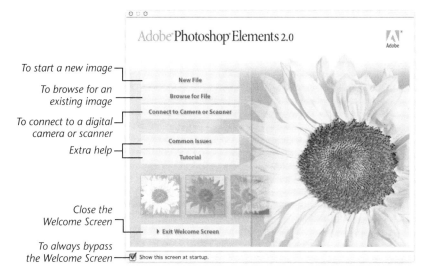

Figure 1-1 *The Welcome Screen is Elements' way of saying, "Hi, what do you want to do?"*

You can see that the Welcome Screen is a pleasant greeting that demonstrates Elements' eagerness to get to work; but let's close it for now and move on to the real meat-and-potatoes stuff. Click the Exit Welcome Screen option to close it.

> **AS A MATTER OF FACT** *If you decide you'd rather not see the Welcome Screen each time you launch Elements, simply click the Show this screen at startup box at the bottom of the Welcome Screen to remove the check mark. Now Elements won't show the Welcome Screen when the software is launched.*

Know the Work Area

Even though we closed the Welcome Screen, there's still a lot of stuff left on your screen. Just what are all those menus, icons, and toolbars? Well, in various ways, this stuff helps you get things done. Collectively, they are called the *work area* (see Figure 1-2), and understanding it is essential to taking full advantage of Elements' many exciting features. It might seem like a lot to master, but there's no need to fear. This chapter will help you make sense of the Work Area. And we'll give you some clues and tips to exploring the work area on your own.

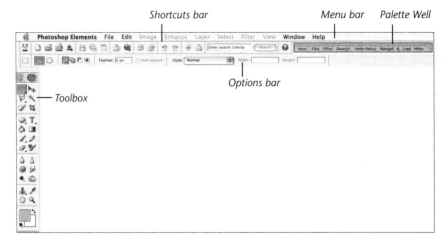

Figure 1-2   *The Work Area is the combination of everything that Elements puts on your screen when you start a work session.*

Open an Image

You know you can open an image with the help of the Welcome Screen, but the more common route is through the File menu. Move your cursor over the word File at the top of your screen and click to see a menu of commands. To open an existing image from your hard drive or a CD-ROM, move your cursor down the menu and click Open. Do that now.

A dialog box appears to help you navigate through the contents of your hard drive and find the file you want to open (for more on this, see Chapter 2). In essence, you're showing Elements where to go to get the image. So we're all on the same page, we'll use a sample image that Elements placed on your hard drive when you installed the program.

1. Through the Open dialog box, find your hard drive and open it.
2. Now find and open the Elements folder.
3. Find and open the Tutorial folder.
4. Select the file named Start.psd and click Open.

The Image Window

You should now see an image of a toy wooden figure on a beach. The area that Elements uses to display the image (any image) is called the Image Window (see Figure 1-3). An Image Window exists for two reasons: to display an image and to provide information about it. As with most things in Elements, you have some control over how your image is displayed and what information it shows you.

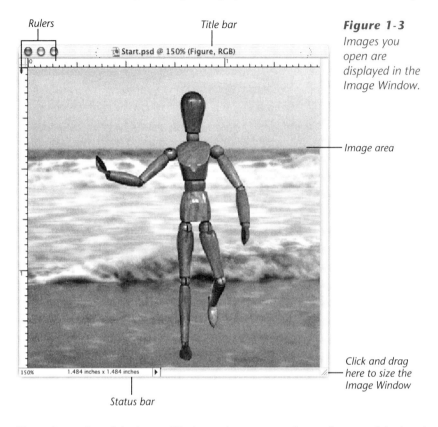

Rulers

Title bar

Start.psd @ 150% (Figure, RGB)

Figure 1-3
Images you open are displayed in the Image Window.

Image area

Click and drag here to size the Image Window

150%   1.484 inches x 1.484 inches

Status bar

The main portion of the Image Window, where you see the toy figure and the beach, is called the *Image Area*. It's where you'll do much of your work: editing, drawing and painting, and selecting pixels. While the Image Area is part of it, the Image Window is much more than just a frame around the image. It also provides valuable information about an image. For example, at the top of the Image Window is the Title bar, which displays the name of a file, the current view's magnification, and its color mode (color modes are explained in Chapter 2). So from a quick glance, you can tell a lot about an open image.

> ***AS A MATTER OF FACT*** *You can use the Title bar to move the Image Window around the Work Area: Place your cursor over the Title bar, then click and hold your mouse button to drag the Image Window to a new location on your screen.*

The Status Bar

The information an Image Window can convey is found not only in the title bar. The bottom of the Image Window, called the *Status bar*, contains more detailed information about a file (see Figure 1-4). It can actually tell you a number of things about your image, such as file size, print size, and even the name of the tool that is currently selected. To see what we mean, click the small triangle located in the Status bar to reveal the pop-up menu of options; these options tell the Status bar what information to display. Choose Current Tool and watch the information on the Status bar change to reveal which tool is currently selected from the Toolbox. Now choose Document Dimensions from the same menu and watch the Status bar change again.

> **AS A MATTER OF FACT**   *Move your cursor over the Status bar (not the triangle), then click and hold your mouse button to see all the vital stats of a file like the pixel dimensions and resolution.*

Figure 1-4
The Status bar's pop-up menu lets you choose what kind of information to display.

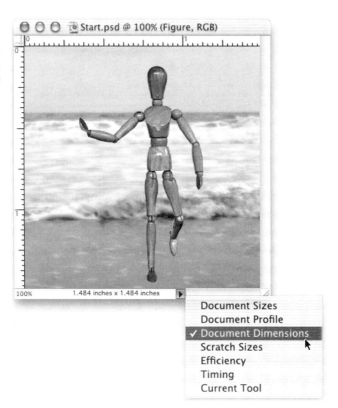

Turn On Rulers

You can also choose to include two helpful features in the Image Window: Rulers and Grid. Both are activated from the View menu. The Rulers are probably already visible along the top and down the left side of your Image Window now, so go to **View | Show Grid** to make the Grid visible as well. Although we like to keep the Rulers on all the time, we turn on the grid only when it's needed (we find it distracting)—to turn off the grid, go back to **View | Hide Grid**. You'll find these features especially useful when you want to align items like text within an image.

Resize an Image Window

Like most windows on a computer screen, the Image Window can be resized at will. You might want to do this, for instance, if you're working with multiple images at the same time. To shrink or expand the window, click and drag the box in the lower-right corner of the Image Window (Mac) or position the cursor just outside the lower-right corner of the Image Window; when a double arrow appears, click and drag (Windows).

Choose Menu Commands

When we opened our image at the beginning of this chapter, we used commands from the Menu bar (that's the series of words running along the top of your screen). When you click one of these words, like we did with File, a drop-down menu appears with a list of commands from which to choose (see Figure 1-5). Try it again: Move the mouse cursor to File, then click. Notice the right-pointing triangles next to some of the items in the list. These point the way to additional commands; they're like menus inside of menus. And when you add them to the mix, you end up with literally dozens and dozens of things you can do, just from the menu commands alone.

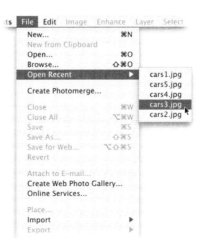

Figure 1-5
Menus inside of menus

View Windows

In time, you'll find yourself using some menus more frequently than others, for instance, the File and Edit menus. That's because they contain the most basic and general commands like Open and Copy and Paste. But don't let them crowd out useful menus like View, Window, and Help. While the commands in the File and Edit menus do something to an *image*, the commands in the View, Window, and Help menus do something to the Work Area, not the image itself.

Retrieve the Welcome Screen

At the beginning of the chapter, we closed the Welcome Screen. But what if we want to get it back? All we have to do is go to **Window | Welcome**. Poof, the Welcome Screen appears. To close it again, return to **Window | Welcome**. See what we mean about how the commands here don't affect the image? The View or Help menus can similarly improve or customize your Work Area.

Change an Image

You now know that some menu commands don't change an image at all. But the majority of menu commands do—they change an image or part of an image. We want to quickly show you a couple of these commands and how they work, so you can see what we mean.

Flip

Have you noticed how commands in the menus are organized? The menu names—Edit, Image, Window—are actually clues to the commands you'll find therein. So you can expect to see commands, say, that have to do with color correction under the Enhance menu. To see how a command can alter an image dramatically, go to **Image | Rotate | Flip Vertical** to turn the toy man on his head.

Rotate

As you can see, menu commands are simple to use. But not all of them make automatic changes; many require user input before a command can be completed. For example, choose **Image | Rotate | Custom**, but don't release the mouse button yet. See the ellipsis? That means that this command requires additional input from you. Now, release your mouse button and a dialog box asks you for some specifics (see Figure 1-6). Elements needs to know how much to rotate the image, so enter a value of 15 in the Angle field, click the Right radio button, and then click OK. Based on these instructions, Elements rotates the image 15 degrees to the right.

Figure 1-6
Some menu commands require user input.

Take a Shortcut

Just below the Menu bar, you should see a row of icons lined up horizontally (see Figure 1-2) to form what's called the Shortcuts bar. It's called this because it provides shortcuts to a handful of commonly used menu commands like Print and Save. For instance, if you want to open an image, you don't have to choose **File | Open**, you can just click the Open icon in the Shortcuts bar; it can eliminate frequent trips to some menu commands.

Step Backward

We think the Step Backward and Step Forward buttons on the Shortcuts bar are invaluable. In fact, we like them so much, we'll have you use them throughout the book. To demonstrate, say we're sorry we rotated and flipped the toy figure image. As you might have guessed, the Step Backward button does just what it says—it takes you back in time. Click the Step Backward button in the Shortcuts bar now (see Figure 1-2), then click it again. See? You just undid the previous two image alterations: rotate and flip. Now hit the Step Forward button two times to restore those transformations (see "Use Palettes" in this chapter for more on "stepping back in time").

Key Commands

But that's not the only shortcut to performing some menu commands. Another option is a *key command*. Click the File menu to see what we mean. See the characters to the right of the Open command? Those characters indicate which keys you need to press simultaneously on your keyboard to access that menu command. They're shortcuts. To open a file, you don't need the menu command or even the shortcut bar; you can just press a combination of keys on your keyboard. And while you certainly don't need to memorize every key combination available, some menu commands, like Open, Save, Print, and Quit, are so common it might be worth the practice. In time, they'll become second nature, and they're guaranteed to improve your efficiency.

> **AS A MATTER OF FACT** Go to **Help | Photoshop Elements Help | Contents | Macintosh (or Windows) Shortcuts** to see a quick reference to shortcuts.

Use Palettes

Just to the right of the Shortcuts bar you'll see what's called the Palette Well. See all the overlapping tabs that look like file folders? Each indicates a palette with a specific purpose. Roll your cursor over each tab to see what we mean. A *palette* is a floating box that can display a range of things from image-editing features to a list of menu commands; and the Palette Well is where they all reside when not in use. Though we can't discuss them all now—you'll learn about specific palettes later on—we will explain some general characteristics common to all palettes and give you a couple of tips to use them efficiently.

View a Palette

To effectively use any palette, you should bring it out of the Palette Well and into the Work Area. To view a palette, just click on its tab in the Palette Well. But if it's a palette you'll use frequently, you might want to pull it out of the Palette Well. To do so, click the Undo History tab and, as you hold your mouse button down, drag the tab down and out of the Palette Well. To move the palette around the Work Area, just grab the tab again and drag it to a new spot. And when you're done with a palette, to keep the Work Area tidy, click the button in the upper-left corner of the palette to close it.

> **AS A MATTER OF FACT** *To resize a palette, click and drag the size box in the lower-right corner of the palette.*

Now let's take a closer look at the Undo History palette and to see why it's one palette we like to have in the Work Area all the time. The Undo History palette displays a list of all the changes, up to a limit, you've made to your image during a current work session; it's a step-by-step record of any transformation. In our case, the Undo History palette shows that we opened an image, flipped it, and then rotated it.

Figure 1-7
The Undo History palette lets you travel back in time.

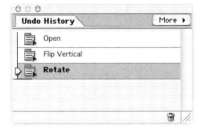

AS A MATTER OF FACT *The Undo History palette clears each time a file is closed.*

The most recent history state is at the bottom of the list. See the little pointer and how Rotate is highlighted in the palette? That indicates which state is active in the Image Window. To return an image to a previous state, click that state in the list on the palette. Better yet, hit the Step Backward button in the Shortcuts bar now and watch the Undo History palette. Essentially, they do the same thing. The benefit of the Undo History palette, however, is that you can see where you're going and you can skip back several stages, rather than one at a time.

AS A MATTER OF FACT *The default number of edits you can undo or redo is 20, although you can change it by going to the General section of the Preferences options. We recommend the default setting, as higher numbers can adversely affect the efficiency of your computer when running Elements.*

Combine Palettes

While we like to keep the Undo History handy at all times, there is a downside to pulling palettes out of the Palette Well: clutter. Use too many at once and you might crowd out your Image Window. You can combine palettes into one unit when you want multiple palettes accessible but don't want to clutter the Work Area.

1. Make sure the Undo History palette is pulled down from the Palette Well.

Click the tabs here to view a hidden palette

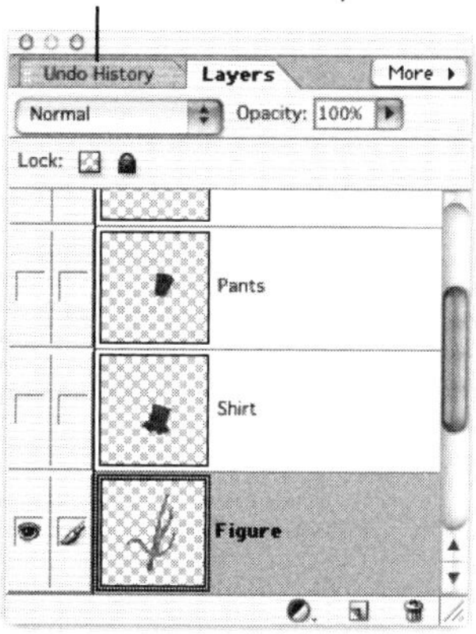

Figure 1-8 *Combine palettes to save space in the Work Area.*

2. Drag the Layers palette down from the Palette Well, beside the Undo History palette.

3. To combine them, grab the Layers palette tab and drag it over the Undo History palette; when you see a black outline around the Undo History palette, let go. You should now see both palette tabs in one palette. You could even add more palettes.

4. Just click the appropriate tab at the top of the palette to switch back and forth.

5. To separate palettes, grab a palette's tab and drag it out of the group.

Dock Palettes

There's another way to save space and organize palettes. You can *dock* one palette to another. Instead of one palette hiding behind another, which is basically what combined palettes do, docked palettes remain visible and separate. We can show you the difference better than we can tell you.

1. Separate the Undo History and Layers palettes (see Step 5 of "Combine Palettes").

2. Grab the Layers palette tab and drag it to the very bottom of the Undo History palette. It's important that you drag the tab to the very bottom—not over the whole palette—otherwise, you'll combine, not dock, the palettes.

3. Release when you see an outline in the bottom bar of the Undo History palette.

So you can see how docked palettes are different from combined palettes. *Combined* palettes behave like they're stacked on top of one another. But *docked* palettes just hang out and go everywhere together.

AS A MATTER OF FACT   *You could even combine two palettes and then dock them to a third palette.*

Figure 1-9
Dock palettes to eliminate clutter.

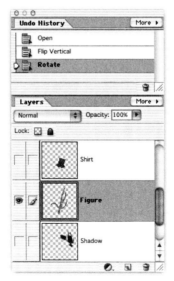

Wield Tools

Like an experienced chef, Elements keeps everything in its place. And the place for Elements' tools is in the Toolbox, of course. You've noticed it by now we're sure; it's that skinny window full of odd-looking icons you see on the left side of your screen. Take a look at it now (see Figure 1-10). It's clear that there's a lot to choose from; the trick, as with any craft, is to know the right tool for the job. To help guide you, the Toolbox is divided into sections: selection tools, creation tools, retouch tools, some miscellaneous tools, and some color features at the bottom.

Select a Tool

Before we jump into the Toolbox, drag the Hints palette down from the Palette Well. We'll talk about this again, but you'll find it especially useful as we talk about the tools. To see what we mean, move your cursor over a tool in the Toolbox and hold it there. Now look at the Hints palette. You should see a brief rundown of that tool's usefulness. Use these Hints to guide your tool choices as you explore and experiment.

To select a tool, click its icon in the Toolbox. A little triangle in the Toolbox indicates that a tool has other, closely related tools hidden behind it. To access these hidden tools, just click the tool icon in the Toolbox and hold down your mouse button until the hidden tool choices appear, then click to select a hidden tool.

Selection Tools

As we said, the tools are grouped together according to their function. The top group of tools, for example, is used to select pixels (see Chapter 4 for more on this). They let you isolate parts of an image for manipulation. What does that mean? For example, if you want to remove the deadbeat boyfriend you just dumped from all of your photographs, you can do so without affecting the rest of the image.

Creation Tools

The tools in the next group are used for drawing, painting, and creating type. They're what you'll use to put a mustache on your sister, paint your own image, or add a funny caption to a vacation snapshot. But there is one tool in this group that really belongs in the next group: the Red Eye Brush. You'll see why in a minute.

Retouch Tools

The retouch group of tools includes some things you might need to improve on a less-than-perfect image. From scratches to fuzzy edges, the tools in this group can help nudge an image into greatness by correcting common flaws, like the demonic red eyes you sometimes get when you use a flash (that's why we think the Red Eye Brush tool belongs here). The uses of these tools are so varied that you'll probably find yourself using them early and often.

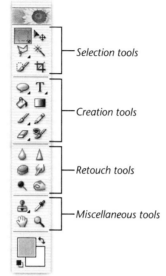

Figure 1-10
The tools in the Toolbox are grouped into loose categories.

Selection tools

Creation tools

Retouch tools

Miscellaneous tools

Miscellaneous Tools and Color

The next-to-last group of tools in the Toolbox is a bit of a hodgepodge, so we're at a loss to categorize them. We actually admire their reluctance to conform and think it makes them the most interesting tools of all. For hints on what they do, see the Hints palette and try them out.

And the bottom section of the Toolbox doesn't really contain tools at all, it contains the Foreground and Background color settings. What you see here comes into play most when you use the paint and draw tools, which you'll hear more about in Chapter 6.

Set Tool Options

See the bar just below the Shortcuts bar at the top of your screen? That's the Options bar and it is most closely associated with the workings of tools. The settings here let you control the behavior of the tools (as well as some menu commands). These settings are dynamic, meaning they change according to the tool you've selected. For instance, select the Rectangular Marquee tool from the upper-left corner of the Toolbox and look at the Options bar. Select the Lasso tool—just below the Rectangular Marquee—and watch the settings in the Options bar change.

> **AS A MATTER OF FACT** *Anytime you select a tool from the Toolbox, be sure to check out the settings in the Options bar before putting the tool to use. This will ensure you get the most out of each tool.*

Change Your View

Now you know a little bit about where to find stuff and how to get around the Work Area. You know what an Image Window is and where to find the tools and palettes. You even used a few menu commands in the process. One could argue that of these things, the Image Window is the most important. It's where you see an image and where you'll do most of your work in Elements. In service of that, we want to show you a few things about how the Image Window works.

Magnify

We already told you how to change the size of the Image Window, to make it bigger or smaller. But now we want to show you how to change the size of the view that's inside the Image Window. We want to magnify the image. You'll find it useful when you need to see an area of your image close-up. Elements gives you a few ways to do this: Enter a value in the lower-left of the Status bar; use the View menu commands; or use keyboard commands as shortcuts. But we're going to show you how to use the Zoom tool to magnify an area of an image.

Zoom Tool

Select the Zoom tool from the lower-right of the Toolbox (it looks like a magnifying glass). It's important to understand that when you zoom in on an area of an image, you're not changing the actual size of the image, just the way that Elements displays it. Simply move the cursor to an area of the Image Window and click once and then once more. Each time you click, the image is magnified—in fact, you could keep clicking until you magnify the image view to 1,600 percent.

> **AS A MATTER OF FACT** *If you want to go straight to maximum magnification, click and drag on a specific area of the image. This will instantly boost the magnification to 1,600 percent and focus on a specific area.*

Figure 1-11
Magnify an image view with the Zoom tool.

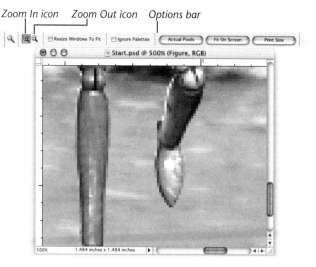

Now look at the Options bar and find the Zoom Out icon (it's on the left side and looks like a magnifying glass with a minus sign). Click it and move the cursor back to the Image Area and click. That's how you minimize your view. Don't forget to try the other buttons that appear in the Options bar when the Zoom tool is active; each one will affect the image view in a unique way.

Navigate the Image Area

Once you zoom in on an image, you'll soon find the need to move to a part of the image that is hidden from view. You can use the Image Window's scroll bars; they're found on the right side and along the bottom of the Image Window, but are visible only when the image is larger than the Image Window. You can also use the hand tool from the Toolbox; click and drag the image around the Image Window. But the best way to navigate an image in the Image Window is from the Navigator palette.

Navigator Palette

Click the Navigator palette tab in the Palette Well and drag it down to the Work Area. What you see in the palette is a thumbnail of your entire image (see Figure 1-12). The red box on the thumbnail indicates the portion of the image that is currently visible in the Image Window. Try this: Position your cursor inside the red box in the Navigator palette then click and drag the red box to another part of the thumbnail. See how the view in the Image Window changed?

For even greater navigation ease, grab the box in the lower-right corner of the palette and drag to make the palette bigger; the thumbnail of your image also grows with the palette, so you can see it better. You should know that, from the

Navigator palette, you can zoom in and zoom out without touching the Zoom tool; the buttons and the slider at the bottom of the palette control this to make this palette a true multitasker.

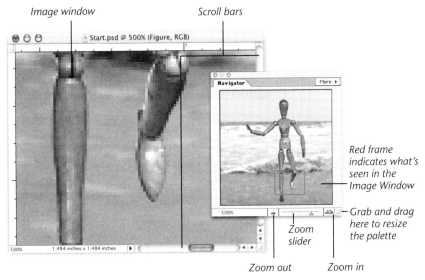

Image window   *Scroll bars*

Red frame indicates what's seen in the Image Window

Grab and drag here to resize the palette

Zoom slider

Zoom out   *Zoom in*

Figure 1-12   *Use the Navigator palette to move around an Image Window when a view is magnified.*

Boost Performance

Now that you're familiar with the Work Area, you might be tempted to dive into one of the more advanced chapters. We don't blame you—making a photograph look like a surrealist painting is exciting. But we hope you'll stick with us a little bit longer because part of understanding Elements is knowing how to maximize its performance. What follows are a few tips to point you in the right direction.

Set Preferences

Application settings called Preferences tell Elements how to handle some general things like the appearance of cursors or the unit of measurement used by the rulers. But a few of these Preferences can also help improve Elements' speed and performance. Let's look at a couple now.

Random Access Memory

As you'll soon learn, Elements is a mighty powerful application. And that means it needs a lot of RAM to perform efficiently. If your computer's light in the RAM department, you'll notice some slow operations and sluggish behavior—especially when performing complicated tasks.

One way to boost Elements performance is to allocate more memory to the program. Choose **Edit | Preferences | Memory & Image Cache**. Then increase the percentage of memory used by Elements (to, say, 75 percent). The new setting will not take effect until you quit and relaunch Elements. But it's important to be careful when allocating additional memory to Elements (or any single application); the more memory you devote to one application (including Elements), the less is available to run other applications at the same time.

Scratch Disks

In addition to increasing the amount of memory allocated to the application, you can tell Elements to use free space from your hard drive as if it were RAM. It's a bit of a shell game, but it works. This is called a Scratch Disk. The default Scratch Disk is always your startup disk, which Elements chooses automatically. But if you have access to more than one disk (if you've partitioned your hard drive, for example), you can choose which disk will be used as a Scratch Disk; in fact, you can assign as many as four. Just keep the following things in mind when assigning Scratch Disks:

- Assign Scratch Disks to drives other than the one you use to edit large Elements files.

- Scratch Disks should not be removable media.

- Drives assigned as Scratch Disks should be defragmented regularly with a disk utility tool like Windows Disk Defragmenter or Norton Speed Disk.

Figure 1-13
Set the Scratch Disk preferences to boost performance.

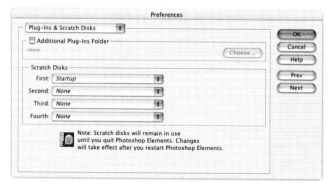

To set Elements' Scratch Disk preferences:

1. Go to **Edit | Preferences | Plug-Ins & Scratch Disks** (Windows and Mac OS9) or **Photoshop Elements | Preferences | Plug-Ins & Scratch Disks** (Mac OSX).

2. Select the target disks from the Scratch Disk menu.

3. Click OK.

4. Restart Elements.

Learn More

We're almost ready to turn you loose, but there's one last fundamental we haven't discussed yet: practice. The more you use and explore all of the features in Elements, the better you'll be at editing images. And the best part is, Elements provides several great features to make practicing both easy and fun. We won't discuss them in detail; we'll simply let you know where to start.

Hints

As you continue to learn about the many tools and features in Elements, we strongly recommend that you always keep the Hints palette visible. We've already mentioned this in the Tool section of the chapter, but it bears repeating.

Pull the Hints palette down from the Palette Well and move your cursor over a tool in the Toolbox. Now look at the Hints palette. You should see some handy information related to that tool. Now move your cursor to one of the palettes in the Palette Well to see how the Hints palette gives you the lowdown on palettes as well. And don't miss the links to Elements Help—they appear in blue on the Hints palette—you'll get more detailed information there.

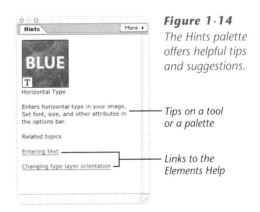

Figure 1-14
The Hints palette offers helpful tips and suggestions.

Tips on a tool or a palette

Links to the Elements Help

How To

As if the helpful Hints weren't enough, there's another palette designed to help you learn more: the How To palette. Go ahead and drag it down from the Palette Well now. You'll see that the How To palette contains a number of simple recipes for getting things done with Elements. It's easy to use; just click the Select a Recipe menu bar, then scroll to one of the topics in the drop-down menu. Click a recipe that interests you and follow the instructions.

While it's no substitute, the How To palette is a great supplement to this book. As much as we'd like to, we simply can't cover everything in detail here. So if you're looking to accomplish something specific and don't find it in these pages, the How To palette is the next place to look.

Help

For more comprehensive information, see the options under the Help menu at the top of your screen. From here, you can launch the Elements Online Help, which opens in a web browser. You should also notice that there's a Glossary available from the Help menu. Use it. And for more directed instruction, try working through some of Elements' tutorials, which is yet another choice from the Help menu. These tutorials will take you step-by-step through some common tasks, because some of us learn best by doing.

Figure 1-15
Access the extra help that Elements offers through the Help menu.

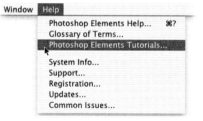

AS A MATTER OF FACT Don't forget to try the Search field in the Shortcuts bar for help. Just type a keyword into the field, click the Search button, then choose from the results.

There's one last place to go for help: the Photoshop Elements page of Adobe's web site, where you'll find downloads, product information, support, and even additional tutorials. And to make it a little easier, Adobe hid a link to the web site in the sunflower image at the top of the Toolbox. Click it and you'll get a direct link to the resources available. It's a fantastic resource, so be sure to check it often.

2

Get Images

Now that you're familiar with where things are, you're probably ready to put Elements to work. Your first order of business is to get your hands on some images by either scanning some traditional photos or taking shots with a digital camera. While we can't help you with the first step, we can show you something about the next step, which is opening those images into Elements.

In fact, this chapter is all about getting images into Elements. The last chapter provided a preview of just how easy it is: Choose an option from the Welcome Screen or from the Menu bar. You did this, for example, to open the image of the toy figure on the beach. But there are other ways to get images into Elements. You can import them directly from a digital camera or scanner or use the handy File Browser. You can even import stills from a video camera or images from a PDF. We'll cover all of these options for starting a work session in Elements.

Apart from showing you how to get an image into Elements, we'll give you the lowdown on the basic technical information you need to know for everyday scenarios. But don't worry. You won't get bogged down with a lot of tech-speak. You'll get just what you need to know to, say, send a photo to friends without tying up the phone line with an hour-long upload. So if you haven't already, get that digital camera out, hook up that scanner, or take a quick look at your hard drive so you know where your existing images are stored.

Understand Images

It's probably not news to you that all images are *not* created equal. That's why an image-editing program like Elements exists in the first place. But digital images do share some common characteristics; once you understand those characteristics, you'll be prepared to choose wisely when you create, edit, and save them for posterity.

Know What Kind

To make things a bit more digestible, it helps to have an image open in front of you. So if you haven't done so already, launch Elements and go to **File | Open**. From the Open dialog box, navigate to find the Elements folder on your hard drive and open it. Now find and open the Tutorials folder (inside the Elements folder). Here you should see a file named Start.psd; select it and click OK. This should open the file we used in Chapter 1—the toy figure on the beach.

Now, the first thing to understand about digital images is that they come in two flavors: *bitmap* (sometimes called a raster image) and *vector*. Some files may even contain both bitmap and vector data. Here's the skinny on each:

Bitmap Images

Bitmap images are made up of lots of little squares of color (or various shades of gray) called *pixels*. Normally, when you look at a bitmap image—if it's a good one—you can't see the individual pixels; they're small enough to blend with one another, to create an illusion of smoothness. But believe us, they're there (see Figure 2-1). To see a pixel, magnify the image to about 1,200 percent using a method we showed you in Chapter 1 (the Zoom tool, for example). See the little squares of color? Those are pixels. Now go back to a 100 percent view of the image. The individual pixels aren't visible anymore. That's why most digital images are bitmap images—digital photos, most scans, and even the paintings you can create with Elements' paint tools—because bitmap images excel at creating the illusion of smoothness and subtle shading.

Figure 2-1
Pixels in bitmap images become visible when magnified.

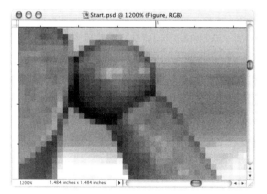

The measure of pixels in a bitmap image is referred to as its *resolution*. Specifically, resolution is the number of pixels it takes to span an inch of the image. The more pixels per inch (ppi), the higher the level of detail in the image. On the flip side, the fewer the pixels, the greater the chance your image will look jagged, rather than smooth. Bitmap images, then, are resolution-*dependent*—their quality depends on their resolution, or how many pixels are packed into an inch of the image. We'll demonstrate this shortly.

Vector Images

Vector images are very different. They aren't created with little squares, they're created using mathematics that only genuine techies and math geniuses understand. The thing to remember about vector graphics is this: They are resolution-*independent*. They're different from bitmap images in this fundamental way: No matter what the resolution or size, they'll always look nice and smooth and crisp when printed. However, the trade-off is that they don't do subtle and smooth shading so well.

Most of the time you'll use bitmap images in Elements. But you can add vector-based graphics to them. Elements uses vector technology to create shapes (see Chapter 7) and type. Which is great, so you get smooth type and crisp circles and squares.

> **AS A MATTER OF FACT**   *Even a vector image will look like square pixels onscreen. That's because your computer monitor can only describe images as pixels. The difference is when you print. Vector images will print crisp and smooth no matter what size you make them. Bitmap images won't.*

The bottom line is this: Because each kind of image (bitmap or vector) has its unique strengths and weaknesses, Elements lets you use both. So you can have the crisp lines of a vector shape and the subtle and smooth shadings in color that a bitmap delivers. You get the best of both worlds.

Change Size and Resolution

Here's why all of this matters. If you know how pixels and resolution work together, when you start fiddling with an image, you can prevent common mistakes that result in crummy-looking images. We know that resolution is a description of the density of pixels in an image. And it's usually expressed as pixels per inch. See the Status bar at the bottom of the Image Window shown in Figure 2-1, where it says "1.484 inches x 1.484 inches"? Move your cursor there now and click to see more detailed information about the file. At the bottom of the list, you should see that the resolution of this image is 225 pixels per inch.

There are two ways to change the size of an image: resizing and resampling. When you resize an image, the number of pixels does not change; rather, the size of each pixel changes. When you resample, each pixel remains the same size, but the number of pixels is increased or decreased. Let's take a closer look at each method.

Resize

Always bear in mind that resolution in Elements is directly related to image size. So when you resize an image, you also change its resolution. To see how this works, go to **Image | Resize | Image Size**. The Image Size dialog box should appear (see Figure 2-2); it displays some of the same information you just saw in Status bar: pixel dimensions, image size, and resolution. Remember that when you *resize* a bitmap image, you actually change the size of pixels. So when you tell Elements to make an image bigger, you actually tell it to do so by stretching the pixels—it now has to make the same number of pixels cover a larger area.

Notice that the number of pixels remains the same

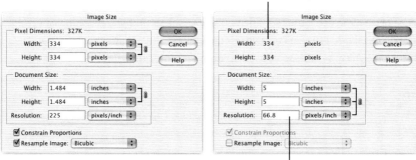

Notice that the larger image now has a lower resolution

Figure 2-2   *The Image Size dialog box, before … and after resizing an image.*

To see what we mean, uncheck the Resample Image box at the bottom of the window. Let's say we want this image to be larger, about 5 inches square. Double-click the Width field and enter a value of 5. Notice that the other two factors (height and resolution) change as well. But most important, you should notice that the Resolution changed to 66.8 pixels per inch. That's because there are still only 334 pixels across. To fill up 5 inches, each pixel now has to grow to fill up that space; it's basic arithmetic. Trust us when we tell you that 66 pixels per inch is bad—it's sure to result in a jagged image and a loss of clarity, so don't click OK.

Let's go in the other direction. Make the width 1 inch. Notice that the resolution increases. That's good if you're concerned with the quality of your image, but you're left with a very small image. So there's a trade-off: When you resize an image larger, you lose quality; when you resize an image smaller, you gain quality.

In the current instance, we're not happy with either of our options, so to clear the settings in the Image Size dialog box, press **OPTION** (Mac) or **ALT** (Windows)—when the Cancel button turns into a Reset button, click it.

Resample

There is a way to get around the size/resolution problem we just demonstrated—sort of. If you want to enlarge your image, but retain a high resolution, you can *resample* an image. Unlike *resizing*, resampling actually changes the number of pixels in the image. To see what we mean, go to **Image | Resize | Image Size.** This time, leave the Resample Image option (near the bottom of the dialog box) checked and set it to Bicubic. Now, type 5 in the Width field, as you did before. See how the pixel dimensions (top of the box) changed and the resolution stayed the same? Elements added pixels; it was 334 pixels and now it's 1125. This is called *upsampling*. Making an image smaller is called *downsampling*, and it removes pixels. So, it looks like resampling solves the resolution problem, right? We can enlarge our image and keep a high resolution and quality. If only it were that easy.

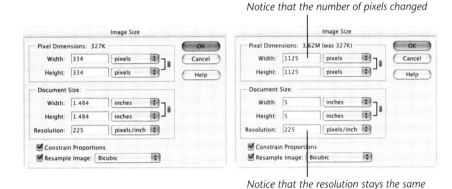

Notice that the number of pixels changed

Notice that the resolution stays the same

Figure 2-3 *The Image Size dialog box, before … and after resampling an image.*

The reality is, upsampling doesn't really work that well. It's nothing more than a sort of cheap cover-up; a bit of a cheat. Generally, our recommendation is to *up*sample only when you're desperate. The bottom line is that resizing and resampling are two different things: Resizing leaves the number of pixels the same, but it affects the resolution; resampling leaves the resolution alone, but it changes the number of pixels.

AS A MATTER OF FACT *Unless you're looking to do weird things to your image, always keep Constrain Proportions checked in the Image Size dialog box. This tells Elements to maintain the image's proportions.*

Go Back to the Drawing Board

So what's the solution? Does this mean you can never enlarge an image? Not exactly. You just have to know what your resolution threshold is. How low are you willing to go in the resolution department?

Fortunately, you can head off size/resolution problems at the pass with some advanced preparation. For example, scan images at a high resolution when possible, say 300dpi; you can always downsize them later. Likewise, if you're taking digital photographs, save them at higher resolutions so you have some latitude when enlarging the images later.

> **AS A MATTER OF FACT**   *Think resolution first: if you're unsure about resizing an image, let Elements do the hard work for you. Go to* **Image | Resize | Image Size***, disable the Resample Image option, and enter a resolution you think is appropriate for the image's end use. Elements will suggest a safe size in return.*

The key is to think about resolution when creating or resizing images. The easiest way to do this is to think about the end use of the image. Will it be posted on a web site, printed from an ink-jet printer, or e-mailed to a friend? If you answer these questions first, then use the list below as general guidelines, you'll end up with images that'll do you proud.

- 200 to 300 pixels per inch to print full-color images or photographs on an ink-jet printer
- 180 to 250 pixels per inch to print black-and-white photos on an ink-jet printer
- 150 pixels per inch to print black-and-white images to a laser printer
- 72 pixels per inch for a web site
- 72 pixels per inch for any image that will be viewed only on a computer monitor

Figure 2-4
The difference between a resolution of 300 pixels per inch and 72 can be dramatic.

300 pixels per inch   *72 pixels per inch*

In summary, just try to remember that a computer screen which displays a resolution of 72 pixels per inch is the low end of the spectrum. And a fancy magazine that's commercially printed is the other end of the spectrum, at 300 pixels per inch. And everything else generally falls between those two ends. So, it's good to know if a photo will be posted on a web site or viewed on a computer screen; then there's no need to save that photo at a resolution that's higher than 72 pixels per inch.

AS A MATTER OF FACT *This resolution thing is a juggling act, because higher resolutions make for larger file sizes; and none of us has unlimited storage space. So you have to plan accordingly and learn to balance the variables.*

Know Color Modes

In addition to being able to control the size and resolution of an image in Elements, you also have the opportunity to determine the number and range of colors that are assigned to pixels by choosing a *color mode*. Elements gives you four choices, which we'll cover in the following sections. The key here, as with resolution, is to know what the end use of an image will be. There's no need, for instance, to save an image in RGB color, if you'll only need black-and-white printouts.

RGB Mode

The most common of the four color modes is RGB, which stands for red, green, and blue. For practical purposes, RGB mode simply means that your image will display and print in color. The more technical explanation is that each pixel in a RGB image is assigned a value on a scale from 0 to 255; this happens for each of the three colors (red, green, blue). So a single pixel actually has three values assigned to it at all times: The first value tells it to display a certain amount of red, the second value tells it how much green to display, and the third value tells it how much blue to display.

But what does all this mean? Well in the end it means that you end up with pretty realistic color overall because, with RGB, there are literally millions of color possibilities. As a result, RGB gives you the most flexibility in terms of color, which makes it the best choice for almost all your color images.

Indexed Color Mode

Indexed Color mode can also be used for color images, but its capabilities are limited. In this mode, the color range is limited to 256 possible colors; that's compared to the millions of colors you can get with RGB. Let's say you convert an RGB image to Indexed Color; this forces Elements to fudge or choose the closest available colors (from the 256)—it has to reassign colors to the individual pixels in an image. So it has to take an image that contains millions of colors and reduce it down to an image that contains only 256 colors. As you can imagine, in most cases, the realistic effect of the RGB color is lost in the translation, which makes it a bad choice for images like photographs or paintings.

Figure 2-5   *The same image in RGB (left) and Indexed Color (right) modes; even if you can't see the color here, you can tell that the Indexed Color image contains far fewer details and shades.*

> **AS A MATTER OF FACT**   *Don't write off Indexed Color completely; it does have its uses. Because it contains so few colors, the file sizes are much smaller than RGB images. For this reason, it's the color mode of choice when preparing images for the Web.*

Grayscale Mode

Grayscale mode is the straight shooter of the bunch; its name says just what it means: shades of gray, 256 to be exact. When you're working with black-and-white images—old photos, for example, or when you know you'll only be printing an image to a black-and-white printer—choose Grayscale mode. Like Indexed Color mode, saving in Grayscale mode will make for a smaller file size.

> **AS A MATTER OF FACT**   *In case you're wondering, you can convert a grayscale or bitmap image to RGB if you like. It won't magically colorize it, but it will allow you to add color to the image with the paintbrush tool for instance.*

Let's convert the toy figure image to a grayscale image now. Go to **Image | Mode | Grayscale** (see Figure 2-6). A dialog box asks if you want to flatten your image, which means that you'd be removing your layers (for more on layers, see Chapter 7).

Just trust us here and click Don't Flatten. You should now see the same image in grayscale; no more color. It's that easy.

> **AS A MATTER OF FACT** *Be sure you really want to convert an RGB to Grayscale or Indexed Color mode before doing so. Once you save and close the converted file, that's it; there's no way to get that rich color back.*

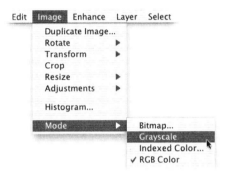

Figure 2-6
Choices from the Image Mode menu

Bitmap Mode

The last of the color mode choices is Bitmap mode (not to be confused with the concept of a *bitmap image*—one has nothing to do with the other). You'll find that you rarely use it because, in Bitmap mode, pixels can only be black or white. Once again, however, Bitmap mode offers an advantage in terms of file size. And, if all you need is black or white, like in line drawings or text, then Bitmap mode is fine.

> **AS A MATTER OF FACT** *You can convert only grayscale images to Bitmap mode. So if you want to convert a color image (RGB or Indexed) to Bitmap mode, first convert it to grayscale, then bitmap.*

Change Canvas Size

So far we've covered some pretty sticky issues. But it'll pay off in the end. Don't worry if you can't remember the specifics of resolution, just experiment on your own. Convert some images to different color modes; change their resolution and print out samples. That's the best way to get familiar with these concepts; hands-on trial and error.

Since you've worked so hard to understand these dicey concepts, we'll throw you a bone and show you how to change the Canvas Size of an image, which is easy. The *canvas* is really just the Image Area—the space on which your image sits. You can think of it as an artist's canvas or a piece of paper. So if you change your canvas size, you're changing only the size of the Work Area, not the size of the image itself.

To see for yourself, choose **Image | Resize | Canvas Size** (see Figure 2-7). Increase the values in the Width and Height fields by about 1 inch. Notice the arrows on a grid at the bottom of the dialog box; that's called the Anchor Grid. Use it to tell Elements where you want your image to appear on the resized canvas. The dark box in the grid indicates your image, and the arrows indicate the direction the canvas will grow or shrink. If you want your image to appear in the lower-right corner of the canvas, for instance, click on the lower-right corner of the Anchor Grid. Then click OK. Go ahead and do that now, to see what we mean.

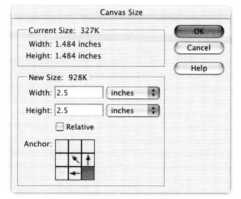

Figure 2-7
Use the Anchor Grid in the Canvas Size dialog box to tell Elements where to put the image on the resized canvas.

Now that your canvas is larger (and your image is in the lower-right corner), you can add other images to the blank canvas or even paint on it. But what about the color of the canvas? When you increase the Canvas Size, the new canvas is filled with the background color that's specified at the bottom of the Toolbox (see Chapter 6 for more about choosing colors). We prefer white, but you can choose any color; just be sure to do it before you open the Canvas Size dialog box.

> **AS A MATTER OF FACT**   If you choose a canvas size that's smaller than the image, it will be cropped or cut off. We don't recommend this, since Elements provides much better ways to crop an image (see Chapter 4).

Open Images

Armed with a basic understanding of image size and resolution, as well as color mode, you now know some of what to expect when you open an image in Elements. You know, for example, that if you want a large printout of an image that's only 2 inches square (and a resolution of 72 pixels per inch), well, you're not going to get very good results. Of course, what you do with an image is your own business—though in later chapters we'll show you many options. But the important thing at the moment is the first step to any work session, how to get your images into Elements. And that's what we'll focus on for the remainder of this chapter.

AS A MATTER OF FACT   *If you know what kind of file you want to open—and you don't see it mentioned in this section—chances are you'll find an option for it in the Files of Type (Windows) or Show (Mac) menu in the Open dialog box. Select the file type form that menu, find the file, and then click Open.*

Open Recent Images

By now you're already familiar with the Open command (from the Menu bar)—you've even used it a couple of times. But you've used it to open the same image each time; and that image happens to be a file that was created in Photoshop Elements—the .psd at the end of its filename tells us that. Right now, we're going to show you how to open other types of files—files that weren't created in Elements. If you haven't done so already, close the toy figure image now: Go to **File | Close** and click Don't Save from the box that pops up.

But wait. Say you've changed your mind and you want the toy figure image open again. You don't have to go to the Open command and find the file again to reopen it; just go to **File | Open Recent** and select Start.psd from the submenu. When you do this you should see how Elements thoughtfully keeps track of the most recent images you opened so you can return to them with ease. This is an especially handy feature if you spend a lot of time working on the same handful of images over and over again.

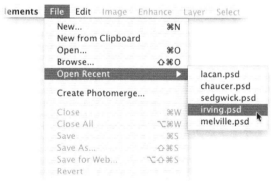

Figure 2-8
If you use the same files frequently, the Open Recent command saves time.

Open Other File Formats

There will probably be lots of times you want to open an image that isn't a native Elements file (as indicated by a .psd), like files from a digital camera. The good news is that Elements can open most file formats you'll encounter with ease. But what's a file format? The short answer is: file formats ensure that particular files comply with the requirements of particular applications. Typically, the file format is indicated by a suffix following a period, as in "Start.psd" or "Melville.jpg". Each of these suffixes clue us in to that file's format. We already know, for instance, that a .psd means the file was created by Elements, so it should open in Elements without a problem. But some file formats can be problematic or even impossible to open. That's rare though; most times, Elements just needs a little help from you.

EPS

If you have a burning desire to know something about each of the file formats, by all means, visit Chapter 9 to get the details. But all we want to do now is show you how to open these files. So it's enough to say here that an EPS file is a common format for files that contain images or graphics and it's an acronym for Encapsulated PostScript file.

To open an EPS file that contains vector data, like an Adobe Illustrator file:

1. Choose **File | Open** and navigate, through the Open dialog box, to the EPS file you want to open.
2. Click Open. The Rasterize Generic EPS dialog box opens.
3. Make sure Constrain Proportions and Anti-aliased are both checked. Constrain proportions maintains the file's height-width ratio. Anti-aliased ensures that jagged edges are smoothed.
4. Elements suggests proper dimensions for the Width and Height—based on the data in the EPS file—but you can change these if you like.
5. Consider the end use of this image, and enter an appropriate value in the Resolution field. The default here is 72, so if you know you'd like to print the image, you should use a higher resolution, like 300.
6. Choose RGB Color or Grayscale from the Mode menu.
7. Click OK.

PDF

You may or may not run across a lot of EPS files, but at some point you're sure to encounter PDF files. PDF stands for a Portable Document Format, and this type of document has become ubiquitous in recent years. That's because just about anybody on any computer can view PDF files—all you need to have is a free program called Adobe Acrobat Reader. In fact, you can find a couple in the Photoshop Elements folder.

But let's say you want to alter a page from a PDF, or maybe you'd like to combine it with other images. Start with steps 1 and 2 of opening an EPS file. At that point, Elements will ask you to select a page from the PDF (if it contains multiple pages). Use the scroll bar or click the Go to Page… button in the dialog box to find the page you want to open, then click OK. From here, it's just like steps 3 through 7 of how to open an EPS.

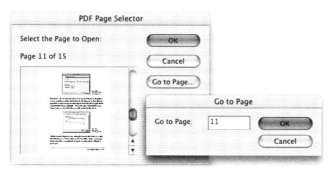

Figure 2-9
When Elements asks, choose a page from the PDF to open.

Photo CD

If you don't own a scanner or a digital camera, you'll find a friend in the Photo CD. Most Kodak film developers offer this option to make your digital life more fulfilling.

In addition to ordering traditional prints, you can also request to have your images converted to digital files that are loaded onto a CD-ROM, which is great, because then you can open them right into Elements with little fuss or bother.

When you get your CD-ROM back from the developer, you'll find that the image files are saved in the PCD file format. To open these PCD files with Elements, first insert the Photo CD into your disk drive. In Elements, choose **File | Open**, navigate to the CD-ROM and select a file, then click Open. Now, you'll need to specify the pixel dimensions and resolution from the dialog box that pops up; consult the section about file size and resolution in this chapter for help with this.

> **AS A MATTER OF FACT** *Can't find a file in the Open dialog box? Select the option to show all files from the Files of Type (Windows) or Show (Mac) menu.*

Browse

There are plenty of other ways to access images files from Elements. The Open command we just showed you isn't always the best option. In the following sections, we'll show you how to use some other commands to get images. But we're going to start with our favorite, which is the Browse feature. Elements' File Browser is like a souped-up version of the Open command we just used. In fact, it's like a file-management application tucked into Elements; you can preview, sort, move, rotate, rename, and delete files all from the File Browser.

The File Browser

You probably noticed that "Browse for File" is an option in the Welcome Window that pops up to greet you each time you start Elements. But you can access it a few other ways: Click the Browse icon in the Shortcuts bar, go to **File | Browse**, or go to **Window | File Browser**. In any case, the File Browser screen appears (see Figure 2-10). You can tell that it's a powerful tool just by looking at it, but don't be intimidated. We'll show you how to get started, then you can explore it on your own.

Let's begin with a little geography, starting in the top-left section of the File Browser window (see Figure 2-10). This first section displays a hierarchical list of the folders on your computer, so it's where you should start your search for an image file. When you find and select a file, the section just below the first section will display a preview of the contents of the selected image file. And the bottom-left section will display detailed information about a the file. The big pane on the right-hand side of the File Browser window shows what's inside a selected folder (in the first section)—you get a quick view of the contents of a folder, not to mention the little thumbnail previews of the contents of the individual files inside that folder.

❶ *Select folder here, to tell Elements where to browse*

❷ *Preview of selected image*

❸ *Detailed information about selected file*

❹ *File information pop-up menu*

❺ *Sort By pop-up menu lets you choose sorting criteria*

❻ *View By pop-up menu lets you choose the file view*

❼ *Shows the number of items in a selected folder*

❽ *Rotate options* **❾** *Trash*

❿ *Select a file here*

⓫ *Press to see the File Browser menu*

⓬ *File Browser menu*

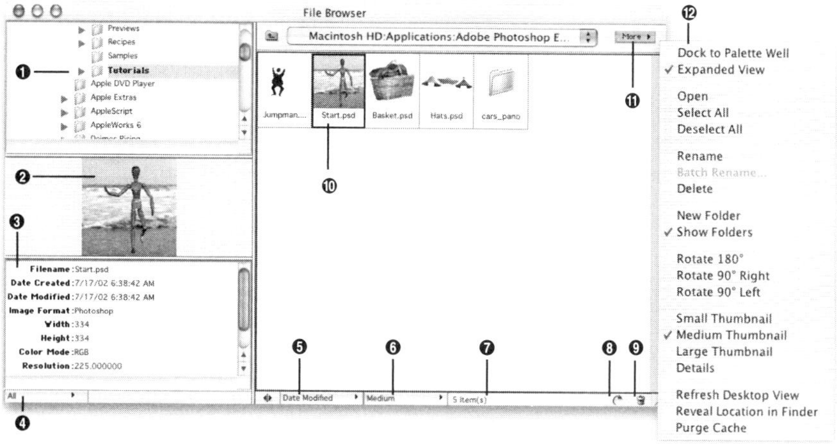

Figure 2-10 *The File Browser screen provides easy access to images.*

Find a File

To browse through your image files, you'll need to start in the top-left pane of the File Browser's window. This section of the window shows a sort of directory of your computer and the folders that are stored there. If you know that you have some images stored in a Folder named "Vacation," for instance, just look for that folder in the directory. When you find and select the folder, you should see the contents of that folder displayed in the big pane on the right side of the File Browser window.

To demonstrate: Find the Photoshop Elements folder on your computer's hard drive, and then find the Tutorials folder and select it. Now look at the right side of the File Browser window. Those are the files (and one folder) that are inside the Tutorials folder. The beauty here is that you don't have to go rooting through countless folders, opening and closing, just to find one or two files.

Customize the Browser

By providing thumbnails of the file contents, the right side of the File Browser window facilitates easy access to a lot of files. To make your access easier still, you can customize the way those thumbnail previews are displayed and organized.

Click on the View By pop-up menu (see Figure 2-10), choose Small, Medium, Large, or Details to change the way the thumbnail previews are displayed. To change how they are sorted in the File Browser window, choose an option from the Sort-By pop-up menu. You can even rotate an image from here if you like: Select one or more of the previews and choose a rotate command from the File Browser menu.

Rename Files

Those nifty thumbnails can also help you do some practical things like rename or organize the files. To rename a file, select its thumbnail in the right pane of the File Browser window, then click the filename, type a new filename, and press **RETURN** (Mac) or **ENTER** (Windows). But if you want to rename a bunch of files, this method could get tedious, so try the Batch Rename command from the File Browser menu. If you own a digital camera, for instance, use the Batch Rename command to change all of those mind-numbingly generic filenames in one fell swoop.

Organize Files

The File Browser can actually preview image files no matter where they are stored—scattered around your hard drive like so many loose socks—but you'll get the most out of the Browser if your images are organized in one location. It could be a folder named "MyImages," for instance. To create a folder with the File Browser, select New Folder from the Image Browser menu (see Figure 2-11) and type in a folder name. Now you can move files into the folder and even make subfolders inside that folder to organize images into more specific categories.

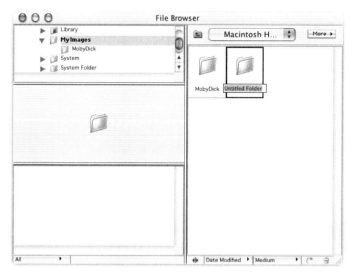

Figure 2-11   *Use folders (and folders inside of folders) to keep your image files organized.*

Connect to a Camera or Scanner

Although we recommend Elements' File Browser to access files, especially if you're in the mood for browsing, it's not always the best option for opening images. If you want to get images from a digital camera or scanner, for instance, you'll probably need to use the Import command.

And if you're not already impressed with Elements, then this should do the trick: Elements can connect directly to a device like a camera or scanner to make opening photos from those devices quick and painless. Of course, if you don't own a camera or scanner, you can skip this section. But we'll bet you get your hands on one or the other soon, after you see how easy image editing is.

> **AS A MATTER OF FACT**   *Digital cameras make it easy to share your images with others. Check out* **Click! The No Nonsense Guide to Digital Cameras** *to get the scoop on how to get the best out of a digital camera.*

Import Photos

You may have noticed that Connect to Camera or Scanner is an option in the Welcome Screen we showed you early on. That's one way to connect to those devices, but we want to show you the Import command, as an alternative. If you own a digital camera but haven't done so already, make sure the software and driver that came with the camera are installed on your computer (consult the manual that came with it). Then make sure the camera is connected to your computer properly.

To get to digital photos from the camera into Elements, go to **File | Import | *your camera's name*.** If you don't see it in the Import submenu, check to make sure the camera's software and drivers are properly installed. If you are able to select your camera's name, the camera's software will launch automatically, so you can select and import the images you want. Once the image is open in Elements, save it as a Photoshop Elements file.

> ***AS A MATTER OF FACT*** *Some cameras "mount" to your computer like an external storage device. If yours is such a case, you may need to access files from the Open or the Browse command, rather than Import.*

Import Scans

Opening a scanned image in Elements is similar to the process we just showed you. Before anything else, make sure your scanner is properly connected to your computer and that any necessary software and drivers are installed. Check the scanner's documentation to see if the scanner has an Elements-compatible plug-in module available; if it does, the scanner's manual should tell you how to install the plug-in. After you install the plug-in module, Elements should be able to open a scan seamlessly: just go to **File | Import | *your scanner's name*.**

Figure 2-12
To connect directly to a scanner from Elements, first load the scanner's software, drivers, and the Elements plug-in module.

> ***AS A MATTER OF FACT*** *Scanners let you create images from almost anything: old photographs, hand tools, fruit—whatever you've got a mind to scan.*

TWAIN

Some digital cameras and scanners use an interface called TWAIN for getting images to your computer (check your scanner's manual). If this is the case with your scanner or camera, you must first install the TWAIN software (check your device's documentation to see how). In most cases, you will have to restart your computer after the TWAIN installation. Then relaunch Elements and go to **File | Import | TWAIN** to connect to the scanner or camera directly.

> **AS A MATTER OF FACT** If your scanner doesn't come with an Elements plug-in module, and TWAIN won't work as an alternative, then use the software that came with the scanner to scan your images and then save them as TIFFs or PICTs; then you'll be able to open them into Elements.

WIA

Those of you using Windows ME or Windows XP can use a utility called Windows Image Acquisition (WIA) Support to import images from some scanners. If you're using WIA, choose **File | Import | WIA Support**. Then follow these steps:

1. Choose the place on your hard drive where'd you like your images to be saved.

2. Click Start.

3. Make sure Open Acquired Images in Photoshop Elements and Unique Subfolder are both checked.

4. Select your scanner.

5. Choose the kind of image you want to scan.

6. Click Preview to see the scan and crop it if you want (you can always crop later in Elements).

7. Click Scan.

Video Stills

If there's a frame in a digital movie (like from a digital video camera) you're especially fond of, Elements can open video stills for editing (see Figure 2-13). The only requirement is that the movies are saved in a format that Elements can read: .avi, .mpg, and .mpeg (Windows) or .mpeg (Mac). To capture an image from video and then open it in Elements:

1. Choose **File | Import | Frame from Video**.

2. Use the Browse button in the Frame from Video dialog to locate the movie.

3. Use the control buttons beneath the display window to play the movie.

4. Use the Grab Frame button to capture the frame(s) you want to save as a still(s).

5. Click Done.

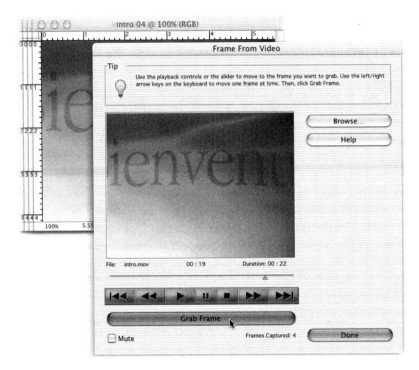

Figure 2-13 *You can even capture still frames from a movie.*

AS A MATTER OF FACT *To ensure it remains editable in Elements, always save imported images in the Photoshop format (.psd). Go to **File | Save** and choose Photoshop from the Format menu. For more on file formats and saving, see Chapter 9.*

This chapter showed you a number of ways to access images and change their size, which are the fundamentals. Now it's time to *do* something to an image. Often, the first step to any image-editing process (after you get the image open) is to make some changes that improve the overall appearance of an image. And that's what we'll show you how to do in the next chapter.

Retouch

We'll assume you've already taken a crack at the first two chapters of this book, so you know how to get around the Work Area and open an image or two. Maybe you got so excited about the possibilities, you got your hands on a nifty digital camera. Or you finally hooked up that scanner. So you click and you scan, and you click and you scan, but the resulting images need a little help. Your kitty's eyes glow red and the vintage photo of your granny looks like it got stuck in the spin cycle. The good news is that fixing these problems is easy in Elements. We'll show you how a few clicks of the mouse can turn red eyes green and nasty old photos crisp and clean.

Digital cameras are great and scanners are useful, but in the end, few images are flawless. There's always some fingertip butting in or a flash that doesn't go off. Elements' answer to the common goofs and failures that plague us all is a specific suite of tools and operations that turn out some impressive improvements. Not enough color in granny's cheeks? No problem, just pump up the color saturation. And what about that cold sore on the groom's lip? A few clicks with the clone tool and adios herpes.

Ours is by no means the last word on the subject, so be sure to check out the Hints and How-Tos that Adobe built into Elements or the scads of web sites that offer advice. In the meantime, get your feet wet with the examples we provide in this chapter and use them as a general guide to explore on your own. We'll discuss some of the most common problems and then show you how to tackle them.

Understand Color

Before we jump in, it's important to understand a few basic concepts of how color works on a computer screen. It's an issue that some people spend years studying, but we'll just cover a few things we think you ought to know, rather than boring you with the technical details. If you want to dig deep into the world of digital color on your own, visit these helpful web sites:

- www.adobe.com/support/techguides/color/colormanagement/main.html
- www.rgbworld.com/color.html
- www.apple.com/creative/resources/color

The Plain Truth

What's most important is the plain truth about color: Color is not color is not color. That is to say, no two devices—digital camera, scanner, printer, computer monitor, or even the human eye—see color the same way. And when you expect these devices to talk to each other about color in the same way, well, things can get a little complicated. In fact, some very smart people have been looking long and hard for a solution to this problem that's easy to apply to our digital lives. And while they've made great strides, the proposed methods vary and the results are unreliable.

If we can agree that becoming a scholar of color theory and a technician in color management—to make all of our devices agree—is unlikely, then we can agree to call close enough *close enough*. Because unless you're dealing with commercial printing or high-end equipment, as far as color goes, close enough *is* close enough. Sure, professionals might see the differences, but for the average Joe or Jane, it all comes out in the wash. That said, it doesn't mean we have to surrender completely to our computers and other digital devices when it comes to color. With minimal effort, we can quiet one squabble in this color tug-of-war: the one between our eyes and our computer monitors.

Calibrate Your Monitor

There are a couple of things you can do to improve the results you get with color in Elements. The first thing is to check your monitor's *color depth setting* (consult your computer's manual) and make sure it's set to display either thousands or millions of colors. If the most your monitor can display is 256 colors, then you might be better off working exclusively with grayscale or black-and-white images, since the range of color your monitor can see is quite limited.

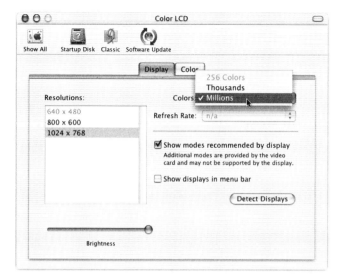

Figure 3-1

To see color more accurately, set your monitor to display thousands or millions of colors.

AS A MATTER OF FACT *Before you calibrate it, make sure your monitor has been on 30 minutes or more to sufficiently warm up.*

Next, you should *calibrate* the computer monitor. By now you know that each link in the chain—eyes, monitor, software, printer, digital camera—has its own way of describing color. The easiest variable to control is the monitor, and calibrating it will help Elements display color consistently, especially if you calibrate your monitor regularly (say, every month or so). To calibrate a monitor, you can use the Adobe Gamma utility that Elements installed on your computer.

AS A MATTER OF FACT *If you're using OSX, you don't need the Adobe Gamma utility; Apple provides its own calibration helper. Find the Display Calibrator utility in the Utilities folder on your hard drive. Double-click it and follow the onscreen instruction.*

Before you use the Adobe Gamma utility, it's good to know that you should calibrate your monitor under the same lighting conditions you normally work in. For instance, if you usually work at night with some lights on, those conditions will affect the way you see the color your monitor displays. So, wait until dark, turn on the lights you normally use, and then calibrate your monitor:

1. Choose **Start | Control Panel** (Windows) or **Apple Menu | Control Panels | Adobe Gamma** (Mac OS9.x).

2. Double-click the Adobe Gamma icon.

3. Select the Step by Step Wizard, click Next, and follow the onscreen instruction.

Figure 3-2
Adobe provides the Gamma utility to help you calibrate your color monitor.

Fix Quick

With a calibrated monitor, you're ready to make corrections to the contrast and color of any image. Of course, Elements provides plenty of ways to fix an image without a lot of fuss, so it's important to be cautious when altering images. Have a plan, because once you start adjusting color and tonal range, it can be the start of a messy chain reaction: make a change to fix a problem and another one pops up somewhere else; fix that problem, all heck breaks loose; in the end, you're left with a mess that's irreparable. Have no fear though, because Elements offers the Quick Fix window, where adjustments are quick and easy. It also combats the chain reaction pitfall, by offering options to undo changes and reset images.

> **AS A MATTER OF FACT** *Don't let the potential pitfalls dampen your enthusiasm to experiment. You can create some great effects by pushing the limits of the things we show you here. So don't be afraid; just be sure you know how to undo a change or make a backup of the original file before you start.*

Quick Fix

Open an image and go to **Enhance | Quick Fix**. Let's say you have an image that's deficient in more than one area: the colors are weak, the contrast is flat, and the details are a little fuzzy. The Quick Fix option makes it easy to improve multiple aspects of an image, all from one window. It even guides you along the way with suggestions and tips. So you can bump up the contrast, nudge the color, and then sharpen the edges to finish the session.

To see what we mean, click the Brightness radio button under Select Adjustment Category (first column) and watch the choices under Select Adjustment (middle column) change. Now select the Brightness/Contrast radio button and watch what happens in the last column. See how each choice you make, from left to right, affects the options available in the next column. You'll learn about things like brightness and contrast in this chapter, but for now, just play in the Quick Fix box to see how it works its magic.

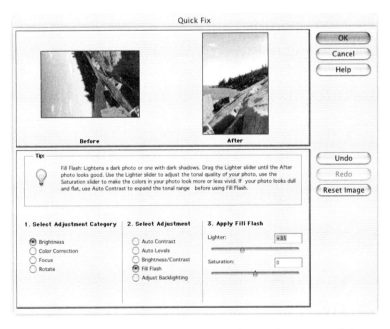

Figure 3-3 *The Quick Fix dialog box rounds up the usual suspects to help you improve images fast.*

> **AS A MATTER OF FACT** *Be sure to read the Tip section in the Quick Fix box; it'll help you make wise choices.*

The Before and After pictures tell the real story here, so if you don't like what you see, click the Undo button. You can use the Undo and Redo buttons, like the Step Backward and Step Forward buttons on the Shortcuts bar. And the Reset Image button takes you all the way back to the beginning of your Quick Fix changes. Use these buttons often to avoid the chain reaction problem we mentioned earlier. In fact, you should always promptly undo any change you don't like, before you move on to other alterations, so it won't affect the preview of subsequent settings.

Now, click Cancel to exit the Quick Fix box and as you move through the rest of this chapter, keep this in mind: Not all image enhancement options can be performed from the Quick Fix dialog box, but the most common ones can, so check it out to see if it works for you.

A Scan

If you're going to retouch and improve a scanned image, there's one thing you should do before color correcting or removing blemishes: If the scan contains white space around the perimeter (maybe it's a crooked as well), go to **Image | Rotate | Straighten and Crop Image**. This command automatically sets your image right and crops out the extra white space. That's important, because that extra bit of white can affect the way Elements sees the overall color in your image.

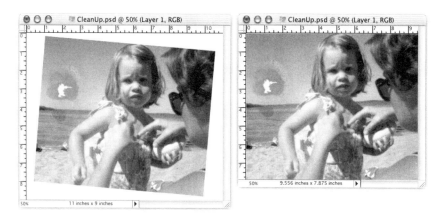

Figure 3-4 *A scan, before … and after the Straighten and Crop Image command.*

Balance Light and Dark

You've probably already caught on to the fact that if you want to do something with Elements, there's usually more than one way to do it. Balancing the light and dark values in an image is no exception to this rule. Some people might refer to it as contrast and others might call it tonal range. Whatever you call it, there's no escaping its influence on all images, black and white or color.

Compensate for Bad Lighting

When you pick up a camera to take a picture, you're often faced with less than ideal lighting conditions. The sun's too bright or the flash didn't go off. Many times you don't even notice these problems until it's too late and you have a photo in your hands. The Adjust Backlighting and Fill Flash commands are Elements' after-the-fact lighting compensators that were built to address these common lighting problems. When you reach for one of the two, it's likely you'll follow up with the other, since the problems they fix often go hand in hand. Each one fixes a specific problem you've seen before: shadows in the foreground that are so dark all detail disappears, and backgrounds so bright that all contrast is washed away.

Fill Flash

Let's try the Fill Flash command first—it addresses the dark blob part of the problem, say a dark shadow on a face in the foreground. Go to **Enhance | Adjust Lighting | Fill Flash**. Remember we mentioned in Chapter 1 how some menu commands need a little help from you to do their stuff? Well, this is one of those instances. A dialog box pops up as if to say, "Give me a hand here, would ya?"

> **AS A MATTER OF FACT**   *Any menu command that requires your input brings up a dialog box. From this dialog box, you can click OK to accept the changes you've made; click Cancel if you want to cancel the change; or click Help if you want to learn more.*

To watch your changes in real time, enable the Preview option just below the Help button. In the Adjust Fill Flash dialog box you see two slider bars. Watch the darkest parts of your image—the shadows—for changes, as you drag the sliders. Drag the top bar to the right to restore detail to dark shadows; and drag the bottom bar in either direction to affect the saturation or intensity of the color in the shadows. Just drag the sliders until you like what you see, then click OK.

Before: Little detail in the shadows   After: More details in the shadows become visible

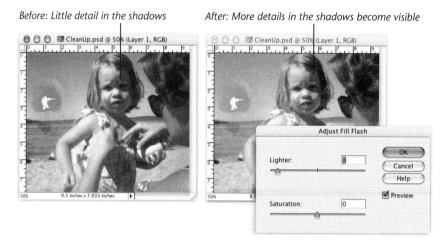

Figure 3-5 *The Adjust Lighting commands help correct poor lighting conditions.*

Adjust Backlighting

For a really bright sky or background, there's nothing better than the Adjust Backlighting command. Go to **Enhance | Adjust Lighting | Adjust Backlighting**. This time you'll see only one slider bar, and it affects the lightest areas of an image. Again, if you make sure the Preview option in the dialog box is enabled, you can watch the changes as you slide the bar around. Click OK when you like what you see.

Improve Contrast

Ever run across an image that needs a little something extra? The tonal ranges are flat so the photo looks drab and lacks contrast between the light and dark values. There are a number of ways to improve the distribution of lights and darks in an image, like through the Auto Levels command. But it lacks refinement and there will be times when you need the more precise control of the regular Levels command.

> **AS A MATTER OF FACT**   *The Auto Levels command can introduce a color-cast to an image. If you use it and notice that your image looks green or blue overall—like a light film of color has been laid over it—undo the command (or use the Step Backward button in the Shortcuts bar) and try the Auto Contrast command instead.*

Levels

As we mentioned, the Levels command will give you a high degree of control over the tonal range of an image. Since that might not mean much to you right now, it's best to just show you how it works. Go to **Enhance | Adjust Brightness/ Contrast | Levels**. In the dialog box that pops up you should see a graph that represents the distribution of light and dark values in the image. This graph is called a histogram. The peaks and valleys on the left side of the graph represent the darkest values, and the peaks and valleys on the right side represent the lightest.

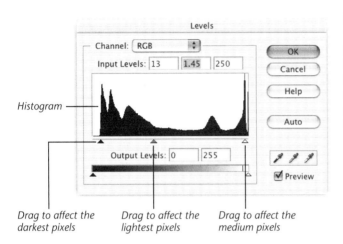

Figure 3-6
The Levels command dialog box lets you adjust the distribution of light and dark values in an image.

The Histogram   So why would you want to know anything about a histogram? Because, right out of the gate, it's a great indicator of whether an image is beyond the help of the Levels command. If the histogram is relatively flat, or there are lots of large gaps, you may have a real turkey on your hands. And while Elements is capable of some amazing things, there are limits to what it can do. To this end, the histogram is a good all-purpose turkey detector. Use it to evaluate whether an image or scan is worth your time. For instance, each time you scan an image, pop open the Levels dialog box and take a peek at the histogram. If it looks and smells like a turkey, then it probably is one and your time will be better spent moving on to another image or rescanning (using different settings).

But if the histogram shows plenty of peaks and valleys, then the image can probably be improved with the Levels command. Here's how: Click the Auto button in the Levels dialog box and watch what happens to the histogram. That Auto button is actually the same as using the Auto Levels command we mentioned earlier—it spreads out the distribution of dark and light values throughout the image. For more flexibility, you can set the levels manually, which is what we'll show you next. But first, hold down **OPTION** (Mac) or **ALT** (Windows) to change the Cancel button to a Reset button and click it now to reset your image.

> **AS A MATTER OF FACT**   *Many dialog boxes don't have a Reset button; press* **OPTION** *(Mac)* **ALT** *(Windows) to turn the Cancel button into a Reset button.*

Adjust the Ends   We explained that the histogram is a road map of the light and dark pixels in your file. To use this road map, you just need to know which end is up. The peak on the far left depicts the darkest pixels in your image (see Figure 3-6). To adjust these darker tones, drag the black triangle (black, for dark) until it sits directly under that peak on the far left. The peak on the far right of the histogram represents the lightest tones in the image. To adjust, grab the white triangle (white, for light) and drag until it lines up with the end of that last peak on the right. There. You just reset the lightest and darkest tones in your image. And although you already see improvements, there's one more thing we should do.

Adjust the Middle   For most images, the majority of pixels fall somewhere in the middle tonal range, between the two ends of the histogram. Since this is the case, adjustments to the midrange often result in the most dramatic improvements. To make an adjustment, grab the gray triangle below the histogram and drag it to the left a bit and watch all those middle-range pixels lighten up. Just move it a little bit—if you go too far, you'll obliterate all midtones from the image. So, small nudges here are best, when you see what you like in the Image Window, click OK to commit to the changes.

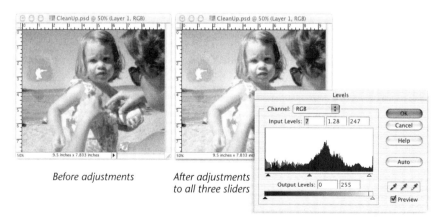

Before adjustments   *After adjustments to all three sliders*

Figure 3-7   *Move the Input sliders on either end of the histogram to see immediate improvements. But the real change comes when you move the middle slider.*

We usually prefer adjusting images manually, like we just did with the Levels command. But there are a few auto options we should mention. For instance, the Auto Levels or Auto Contrast commands (both are choices under the Enhance menu) are capable of improving the tonal range in an image when you're pressed for time. Or you can try **Image | Adjustments | Equalize** for a similar effect. However, you might find (if your image is in fair shape already) that these auto commands have no visible effect on your image. It's not the last word, it just means you'll have to make the adjustments manually.

Correct Color

After you establish a sturdy base—a good balance of light and dark values—it's time to address color concerns. Maybe you scanned a color photo that has yellowed with age. Or maybe the lighting was such that it washed out the vibrancy of the colors. Whatever the case, any adjustment to the color of an image is bound to have a big impact. After all, color is what helps us all understand and describe the physical world around us.

Remove a Color-Cast

We've already mentioned a couple of scenarios involving color-cast: The Auto Levels command can create one in an image, or the colors in a photo can yellow with age. Sometimes a color-cast might be desirable: yellow to make a new image appear old, or blue to make it look cold. But usually, you'll want to rid your images of noticeable color-casts. Elements offers a couple of options to do just that.

Color-Cast Command

The quickest way to remove a color-cast is to go to **Enhance | Adjust Color | Color Cast** and follow the instructions you see in the dialog box that pops up. It tells you to click on an area of the image that should be white or black or gray. You'll probably find it easiest to indentify the lightest part of an image and click on it. Make sure the Preview option in the dialog box is enabled, so you can watch the changes as they occur. If you don't like what you see, click Reset and try again or click Cancel and try another option (next section). If you like the results you see, click OK.

Color Variations

For greater control over the color-cast in an image, go to **Enhance | Adjust Color | Color Variations** to open the Color Variations dialog box. This dialog box is similar to the Quick Fix box—you should see a Tip, as well as Before and After previews. Use these features to guide your choices.

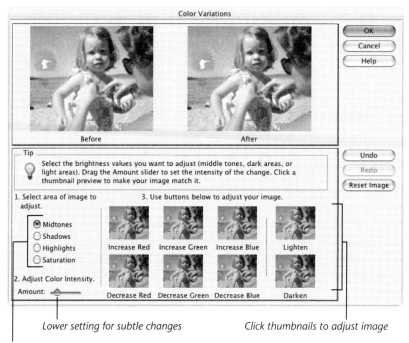

Lower setting for subtle changes   *Click thumbnails to adjust image*

Choose a specific value (light to dark) to adjust

Figure 3-8 *Use the Color Variations box to make color corrections.*

In this one box, you can add or subtract colors from the lightest (Highlights), darkest (Shadows), and middle (Midtones) values of an image. You can also increase or decrease the amount of saturation in the colors that are present—increase the saturation for more vibrant colors.

Say, for instance, that your image has a yellowish tinge to it. First, drag the Amount slider to the left a bit so you can make more subtle adjustments. Then, select the Midtones radio button and click the Decrease Blue thumbnail. That alone might be enough to correct the problem. If it's not, click the Decrease Blue thumbnail again, or switch to the Highlights option and click the Decrease Blue thumbnail again.

Then do the same for the Shadows option. You can even try other adjustments, like the Saturation option.

If, at any time, you don't like a change, simply click the Undo button. Or to revert back to the beginning, click Reset Image. Do and undo until you like what you see in the After preview, then click OK to accept the changes. And that's it.

Improve Color Balance

You can see how the Color Variations box is a quick way to adjust the color in an image. Use it whenever you need to adjust color, whether to remove a color-cast or to make minor adjustments to the color saturation in an image. But you might want to see a more immediate change from time to time. While we don't recommend it often, the Auto Color Correct command can sometimes offer just enough improvement in the color department.

Auto Color Correct

The Auto Color Correction command is the most unpredictable of the auto commands, which makes it impractical, in general. If you know what you want, make color specific corrections on your own, like with the Color Variations box we just showed you.

But if you're open to any possibility, by all means try it. For instance, we used the Auto Color Correction command on a photo of blue sky and clouds and we got a beautiful teal-colored sky—not realistic, but visually stunning. To try it, go to **Enhance | Auto Color Correction** and see what happens. If you don't like the results, click the Step Backward button in the Shortcuts bar to undo the change.

Enhance Color

Let's say you just want to enhance the overall color of an image. Maybe it's a bit washed-out, so the reds are soft and the blues don't sing. Or maybe the adjustments you made to the Levels left the color a little flat. Now you need to enhance the color or increase the saturation. It's a great way to improve images quickly. And sometimes it's just plain necessary.

Saturation

The quickest way to do this is to go to **Enhance | Adjust Color | Hue/ Saturation**. In the dialog box that appears, make sure the Preview option is checked, and Master is selected from the Edit pop-up menu—this tells Elements to edit *all* colors in a file. Grab the Saturation slider and drag it to the right, to a setting of 20 or so, to make the colors more vibrant—adjust it until you like what you see, then click OK to accept the changes.

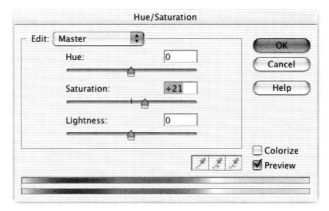

Figure 3-9
Drag the Saturation slider to the right to make colors more vibrant.

> **AS A MATTER OF FACT** To enhance the saturation of a targeted spot, try the Sponge tool and set the Mode (in the Options bar) to Saturate.

Hue

You can use the same dialog box to adjust or enhance specific colors in an image. Go to **Enhance | Adjust Color | Hue/Saturation** and click the Edit pop-up menu (Master) to see the other choices available. Choose a specific color here, like Red, so we can show you what it does. Now drag the Hue slider either left or right, and watch your image. See how it actually changes the colors in your image? But notice how it changes only some colors—if you choose Red from the Edit pop-up menu, then only reds are affected, for instance. So, with the Hue Saturation command, you could make the reds in an image a little more orange, or the blues a little more green. You could also use the Saturation slider to boost the saturation of each color.

> **AS A MATTER OF FACT** These changes accumulate, so if you want to change a second set of colors, just go back to the Edit pop-up menu, choose another color, and drag the Hue slider again.

More Flexibility

For the ultimate flexibility when adjusting the color in an image, try an Adjustment Layer. The advantage of any adjustment layer is that it lets you perform alterations to an image without really altering the original image. You'll see what we mean in a minute, and for a better understanding of layers, you can see Chapter 7.

To enhance a specific range of colors in an image with an adjustment layer, first pull the Layers palette down from the Palette Well.

1. Go to **Layer | New Adjustment Layer | Hue/Saturation** to add an adjustment layer to your file. Click OK when the New Layer dialog box appears.

Figure 3-10
Choose the kind of changes you'd like your adjustment layer to perform.

2. Make the desired Hue or Saturation adjustments (as discussed in the previous sections of this chapter).

3. Click OK to accept the changes when you're ready. See the new layer in the Layers palette? That's the adjustment layer you just made.

4. If you want to view a before and after of your image, simply click the eye icon next to the Adjustment layer in the Layers palette—this will turn off the adjustment layer, so you can see your original image.

5. If you don't like the change, select the adjustment layer's name in the Layers palette, click on the More button in the upper-right of the palette, and select Delete Layer.

AS A MATTER OF FACT You could balance the lights and darks in an image with an Adjustment Layer; just choose Levels instead of Hue/Saturation from the Layers | Adjustment Layers menu.

Fix Flaws

Now you know how to make some general improvements to the color and contrast of an image, which is a vital first step. So, when you open an image, first go to the Enhance menu and employ a few commands to improve your images. Eventually you'll encounter more noticeable flaws in an image, like a scratch. For these, a little tool wielding is required, so we'll show the basics of these repairs in the following sections.

No More Red Eye

The red eye we're talking about here has been around since color film and flash bulbs met, leaving countless ruined photos in the wake. It would be great to nip the red-eye devil in the bud, but unless you have a fancy flash that's built for such challenges, it's bound to strike occasionally. You're in luck, though. Elements has an effective solution in the Red Eye Brush.

Red Eye Brush

The Red Eye Brush changes the color in a specific area—the area that you brush—without changing any of the details in the image. So, you can remove the red in the pupil of an eye without removing any detail. In fact, you could use it to touch an image in areas other than a red eye, like changing the color of an apple from red to blue, for instance. But it primary use is to remove red eyes from flash photos.

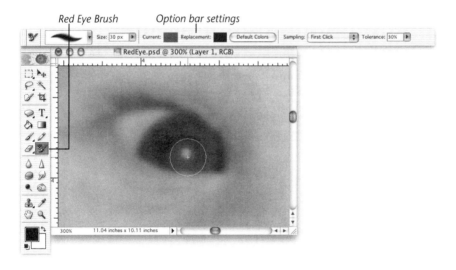

Figure 3-11 *Using the Red Eye Brush is a snap.*

To use the Red Eye Brush to remove red eye from photos:

1. Open the image and zoom in on a red eye, so you can see the details. For help with zooming, see Chapter 1.

2. Select the Red Eye Brush from the Toolbox (see Figure 3-11), then select a brush from the pop-up menu and adjust the size (see Chapter 6 for help with paintbrushes). Select a brush size that's close to the size of the pupil.

3. Set the other Options bar settings: Click the Default button to set the Current and Replacement color swatches; set the Sampling option to First Click; set the Tolerance level to 30 or so.

4. Click directly on the red part of the eye and drag the brush around the area. The red should be replaced with dark gray, but if it's not working effectively, use the Step Backward button in the Shortcuts bar and try again (use different Options bar settings).

AS A MATTER OF FACT *If the results of the Red Eye tool are a little too light—the default color it uses to replace the red isn't quite black—go back and darken the area with the Burn tool.*

Cover-Up

There may be times when you need to get rid of some specks and blemishes on an image. One way to touch up problem areas—whether dust, scratch, or even a cold sore—is to try the Smudge tool (it looks like a pointing finger), because it lets you move or smudge pixels together. You can try it now if you like, or find out more about it in Chapter 6.

Smudge

Select the Smudge tool then click and drag on an area of your image. See how it smears the pixels? You can affect a large or small area of pixels by selecting a large or small brush from the Options bar. Change the Strength setting in the Options bar to control the intensity of the smudge. For small blemishes, start with a small brush and a light intensity.

Clone Tool

While the Smudge tool works fine for cleaning up a few tiny blemishes, we prefer the Clone Stamp tool (see Figure 3-12) for covering more serious imperfections in an image. Select it now from the Toolbox and then take a look at the Options bar. You first need to specify a brush tip from the Brushes pop-up menu and then set the brush size, as you did for the Red Eye brush. Try a regular round brush tip and a smallish brush size (about 5) to start—you can adjust the size later if you need to. Be sure to enable the Align option in the Options bar and then set the Opacity to 90.

AS A MATTER OF FACT *Play with the Opacity setting of the Clone tool; use lower settings and reset the sample point often to create more subtle repairs.*

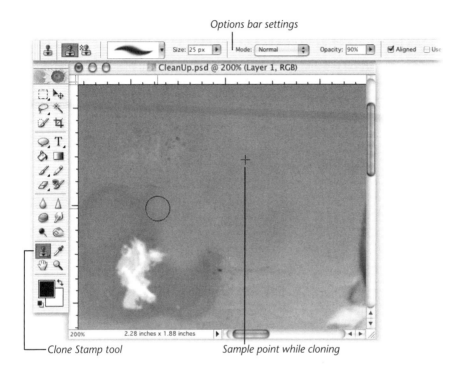

Clone Stamp tool *Sample point while cloning*

Figure 3-12 *Use the Clone Stamp tool to repair damage.*

Once the Option bar settings are addressed, you can put the Clone tool to work:

1. Zoom in to get a close view of the blemish you want to repair.

2. Hold down **OPTION** (Mac) or **ALT** (Windows), position the cursor over an area of the image that's similar in color and tone, and click once to specify a sample point—the tool will clone from sample point to cover the blemish.

3. Now reposition the cursor over the blemish and click once or twice to repair it. You can also click and drag to cover larger areas.

It's easy to get carried away with this tool, but try to keep your enthusiasm in check and cover only what's absolutely necessary, while using a light touch. Otherwise, you'll end up with an unnatural-looking mess, which may look worse than what you set out to fix.

> **AS A MATTER OF FACT**   *If you need to repair large areas, stop cloning occasionally to reset the sample point—hold down* **OPTION** *(Mac) or* **ALT** *(Windows) and click. This helps mix it up, so large cloned surfaces don't end up looking obviously cloned.*

Fine-Tune

So you now know how to make general improvements to the color and contrast of an image, as well as how to hide some flaws. Those skills will improve with some practice. But there are a couple more useful and quick changes that will benefit most images—and you don't need much practice to master them.

Sharpen Details

Every image is a candidate for a little boost to the details. Regardless of how the image got to Elements, any kind of photography degrades the details in an image, it's just the nature of the beast. We'll show you two solutions to this common problem, but first we should point out that, while you can boost the details in an image, you can't work miracles; there are limits to the magic Elements can work, and really blurry images simply can't be fixed. But if you have an image that needs just a little bit of help (most images do), it's a cinch.

Unsharp Mask

Though you wouldn't guess it from the name, the Unsharp Mask filter actually *sharpens* details in an image. And it's such a useful filter, you should probably use it on any image you open into Elements for the first time. Just train yourself to think of the Unsharp Mask filter as an extension of the Open or Import command—open or import an image, then automatically go to the Unsharp Mask filter.

The great thing about this filter is it gives you precise control over its effects, unlike the Sharpen or Sharpen Edges filters, which operate automatically. To try it, go to **Filter | Sharpen | Unsharp Mask**. Drag the Amount slider to the right to set the amount of sharpening that will be applied to pixels. This does just what it says: it controls the amount of sharpening. So the higher the number, the more it sharpens. Try a setting of 100 or so to start.

To tell the filter how many pixels it should affect, drag the Radius slider to a low setting of about 1. This forces the filter to be selective about which pixels it affects, which is good. A higher setting (anything more than 1.5 or so) will allow the filter to be promiscuous, which generally produces bad results like lots of white specs and edges on objects that look like they could inflict serious wounds.

> **AS A MATTER OF FACT** *Move the cursor over the detail of the image in the dialog box, then click and hold. See the image detail change? That's how the image looks without the Unsharp Mask filter; it's like having a "Before" picture. This before and after trick works in many dialog boxes that contain previews.*

Figure 3-13
Too much of a good thing produces unnatural results.

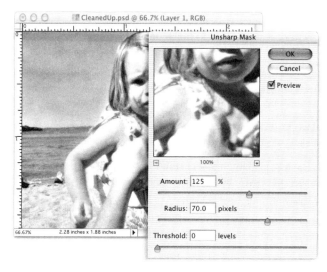

We recommend you leave the last setting in the dialog box (Threshold) set to 0 all of the time, because any other value (especially high ones) essentially cancels out the other two settings. So leave it alone, and if you like the preview you see, go ahead and click OK to accept the filter's changes.

Pin-Point Sharpen

But maybe you don't want to sharpen the details of an entire image; you just want to sharpen a few specific areas, like an eye or a hand. The Sharpen tool makes it easy to target specific areas of an image, because it works like the Red Eye Brush or the Clone Stamp tool; you drag it over specific pixels.

To select the Sharpen tool, look for the button that looks like a triangle (just above the Smudge tool in the Toolbox) and click it. As you did with the Red Eye Brush and the Clone Stamp tool, you should first specify a brush tip and brush size from the Options bar, then set the Strength to 10 or 15. Now you can click and drag over specific areas of an image, to target the effects of the Sharpen tool.

Soften Harsh Edges

Since we want to be fair and balanced, there's one last tool we'd like to show you in this chapter, the Blur tool. It's fair to say that you'll find it just as helpful as the Sharpen tool we just showed you. Sure, you can use the various Blur *filters* to blur all the pixels in an image at once, but the Blur tool can target those effects to a specific area of an image, just as the Sharpen tool can.

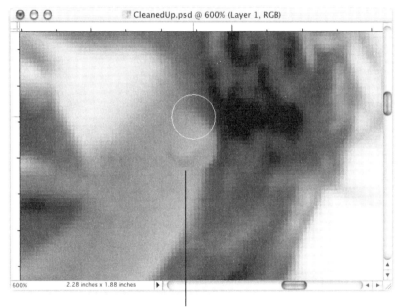

This cloned area left a noticeable edge,
so we'll soften it with the Blur tool

Figure 3-14 *A targeted blur can help enhance or camouflage areas of a photo.*

Blur Tool

Figure 3-14 shows you how the Blur tool can camouflage a cloned patch, to make it less noticeable. But you could use the Blur tool on the entire background of an image, to make the foreground appear more focused, by comparison. You can even use it to soften the wrinkles on a face. To try the Blur tool, no matter the circumstances:

1. Select the Blur tool from the Toolbox (it looks like a drop of water).

2. Set the tool options in the Options bar: Pick a brush tip; set its size; specify a Strength setting (try 10 or 15, to start).

3. Click and drag over the areas you want to soften.

4. If it softens too much or too little, click the Step Backward button in the Shortcuts bar, reset the tool options in the Options bar, and try again.

We showed you how to improve images in this chapter—a touch-up here and a color correction there—to spruce them up. It could be the end of the line, if all you want is better-looking images. But in the chapters that follow, we'll show you how to take these improved images a step or two further by adding text, working with layers, or creating a slide show that you can share with friends.

Select

In the last chapter we showed you how to make global changes to an image that affect all its pixels. This is the perfect way to fine-tune and touch up an image that needs some overall help. There will be times, however, when you want to change isolated parts of an image. To do that, you have to learn how to make selections, which show Elements the specific pixels you want to change.

If you've used a word processing program, you already know how to make a selection of sorts: You use a cursor to select characters or words before editing. In Elements, you use selection tools to select pixels that you want to edit. Say, for instance, you want to change the color of just the cap on Sally's head without changing all of the colors in the picture. You can do that, but first you have to make a selection to tell Elements *where* the hat is in the image. That's what we'll show you in this chapter: how to select pixels.

Crop an Image

A crop is one of the most important transformations you can make to an image. In fact, cropping is so important to image-editing that Elements provides a tool built for just such a transformation, the Crop tool. To perform a crop, you first have to select the pixels in the image you want to keep, then you tell Elements to discard everything else.

Crop Tool

To start, open an image and select the Crop tool from the Toolbox (see Figure 4-1). Position the Crop tool near the upper-left corner of the image, then click and hold the mouse button as you drag toward the lower-right corner. There's no need to worry about getting the crop perfect; we'll adjust it later.

Figure 4-1 *Define a crop with the Crop tool.*

> **AS A MATTER OF FACT** *Unless you're familiar with image resolution and resizing, we suggest you always leave the Options bar value fields blank when using the Crop tool. Just click the Clear button in the Options bar before making a selection with the Crop tool.*

By making a selection with the Crop tool, you isolated part of your image. The line of *marching ants* you now see on the image indicates a *selection border,* which is how Elements shows you which pixels are currently selected. In fact, when you use any selection tool, like the Marquee or the Crop tool, you'll end up with a selection border.

But a selection made with the Crop tool has something extra going for it. Its selection borders get a big bonus in something that's called the *Shield,* which teams up with a selection border to help you visualize a crop ahead of time. When the Shield option is in use, the unselected portions of the image are *shield*ed (or darkened) from view. To make sure the Shield is activated, go to the Options bar and check the Shield cropped area check box.

Figure 4-2 *The Shield helps visualize the crop before you commit to it.*

Adjust the Crop

You should now see how the Shield helps you visualize a crop. We can't imagine adjusting a crop without using it and ours tells us we have a little work to do. We need to move our crop to the right a bit and change its size. You'll soon see how selections made with the Crop tool offer unmatched flexibility, so you can get a crop just right before committing to it.

Use the handles (little squares) on the selection border to stretch and shrink a crop to any size you like. Next, position the cursor *inside* the selection border, then click and drag to move the selection border to a new position on the image (the Shield will move with it). Don't be timid; go ahead and resize and move it around until you're sure you'll like the end results of the crop.

Resizing and repositioning the crop is great, but it's not the only flexibility you're afforded when you use the Crop tool—you can also rotate a crop: Position the cursor outside the selection border, but close to a corner (until you see the cursor change to a curved double arrow). Click and drag to rotate, until you're satisfied with the adjustments, then click the Commit icon on the Options bar.

Figure 4-3 *Rotate a crop.*

Make a Simple Selection

You just learned that to crop an image, you first have to make a selection. In that case, you used the Crop tool, but the Crop tool is only one of several tools that make selections that are simple in shape, like a rectangle. The Rectangular Marquee tool, for instance, does just what its name implies: It makes a selection border that's rectangular in shape. If you need a simple selection in the shape of a circle, try the Elliptical Marquee tool.

Choose the Rectangular Marquee tool from the Toolbox and position the cursor anywhere on your image, then click and drag. When you let go of the mouse button you should see the marching ants that indicate a selection border. To further illustrate, press **DELETE** now to delete the selected pixels. That's what a selection does for you—it makes it possible to do just about anything to the selected pixels: delete, copy, distort, scale, rotate, paint, or apply a filter.

AS A MATTER OF FACT   *To constrain the selection to the proportions of a square or a circle, hold **SHIFT** as you drag to select an area with the Rectangular or Elliptical Marquee tool.*

Make an Irregular Selection

Not everything in the world is shaped like rectangles and circles, so you'll need to be familiar with tools that select irregular shapes, like the Lassos, the Magic Wand, and the Selection Brush. With experience, you'll know how to choose the right tool for the job at hand. You might even find that a combination of tools works best for many situations you encounter. Whichever selection tool you choose, the basic procedure is generally the same: Set the options, make a selection, modify the selection, then do something to the pixels within the selection.

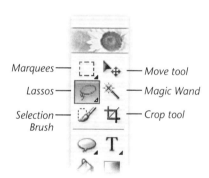

Figure 4-4   *The selection tools you'll find in the Elements Toolbox*

In our example, we want to copy the dandelion seen in Figure 4-1. And since the dandelion is an irregular shape, the Marquee tools won't do the job, so we'll use the Lasso tool. To follow along, open an image that contains something you can copy and click the Lasso tool icon in the Toolbox.

AS A MATTER OF FACT   *Many of the images used throughout this book can be found in a folder called Stock Art on the Elements install CD-ROM.*

Set Lasso Options

With the Lasso tool selected, you should notice a new set of options in the Options bar. This is important because as you experiment with selection tools, you'll quickly learn that those settings control how a tool works. This is what we'll show you next.

Selection Mode

Each time you hunker down to start a selection, remember to click the New Selection button in the Options bar first (see Figure 4-6). This tells Elements that you want to start a brand-new selection, rather than modify an existing one—we'll cover the other buttons here later in the chapter, so you can learn how to modify a selection, such as adding to or subtracting from it.

Anti-Alias

When the Anti-aliased box in the Options bar is checked, Elements will smooth the jagged edges that are common to curved selections, so we recommend you use the Anti-aliased option whenever it's available. To see why, turn off the Anti-aliased option and make a selection with the Elliptical Marquee tool (it's a hidden behind the Rectangular Marquee tool in the Toolbox). Go to **Edit | Fill** and click OK, then zoom in on what you just did to see the resulting jagged edges. Jagged edges are always undesirable, so go ahead and turn the Anti-aliased option back on now.

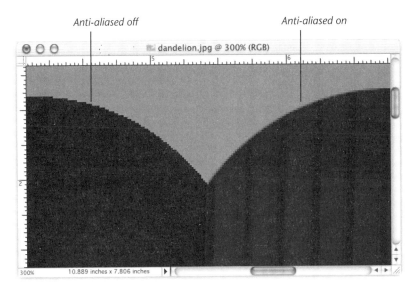

Figure 4-5 *Use the Anti-aliased option to prevent jagged edges.*

Feather

Click the Step Backward button in the Shortcuts bar to undo the damage we did in the preceding section, then select the Lasso tool from the Toolbox again. Now, notice the Feather setting in the Options bar. The number here correlates to the softness of an edge. A high number of, say, 50 makes for a much softer edge than 2. So while a fuzzy edge might be desirable on occasion, you'll get good results with a setting of 1 or so for general use. This low setting will just barely soften the edges of a selection, to make it look more natural than the sharp edge you'd get with a setting of 0.

Use the Lasso

You'll do just fine while using the Lasso tool if you think of it like drawing with a pencil. To try it, click the New Selection button and position the Lasso tool's cursor where you want to start a selection. Then hold the mouse button down as you trace along the edges of the object you want to select. It's just like tracing a picture with a pencil, except the trick here is to end up back where you started, or at least close to it. If you don't return to your starting point (to close the gap) before releasing the mouse button, the Lasso tool will finish the selection for you by making a beeline back to point A. Sometimes this is helpful and sometimes it's a nuisance. Either way, it's never a disaster because we will show you how to improve on your initial selections.

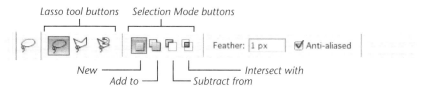

Figure 4-6 *The Options bar settings for the Lasso tool control the appearance of its selection edge.*

Take our selection of the dandelion for instance. It's far from perfect, since we included too much background in some areas around the stem, and we let go of the mouse button too soon, so the top of the dandelion is chopped off. Fortunately, we don't have to start over. We can just add to or subtract from our selection.

> **AS A MATTER OF FACT** *Click anywhere in the Image Area to deselect a selection. If you do so mistakenly, use the Step Backward button in the Shortcuts bar to get the selection back.*

Add to a Selection

Even seasoned pros make sloppy selections. It comes with the territory, so don't sweat it. Besides, as you'll find out in the coming sections, Elements lets you add to or subtract from current selections so you can fix the inevitable flaws. The real advantage here is that you don't have to start over when you screw up an initial selection; just amend and revise it. For instance, to fix our selection of the dandelion, we can add pixels to our existing selection by clicking the Add To Selection button in the Options bar (see Figure 4-6). This tells Elements that you want to *add* pixels to the current selection.

> **AS A MATTER OF FACT** *If you forget to click the Add To Selection button, your current selection will disappear as soon as you click the mouse button. If this happens, try the Step Backward button in the Shortcuts bar to get the selection back.*

Although we used the Lasso tool to make our first selection, we can now use any other selection tool to add to that selection. Even if your first selection was perfect, follow along with us so you can see what we mean. We want to add the top of the dandelion to our selection. And since the dandelion is round-ish, we'll switch to the Elliptical Marquee tool since we know it can make a round-ish selection. The Elliptical Marquee tool is hidden behind the Rectangular Marquee icon in the Toolbox, so click the Rectangular Marquee icon and hold the mouse button until you see the hidden tool choices appear, then click the Elliptical Marquee icon. Now check the Options bar to make sure the Anti-aliased option is turned on, and make sure the Feather setting is the same value you used for the initial selection (we used a Feather setting of 1). Click and drag the Elliptical Marquee's cursor to add pixels to the current selection. Continue to click and drag as many times as you like. In fact, you don't even have to select pixels that are contiguous (next to one another). And don't worry if you include too much; we'll show you how to subtract pixels from a selection later.

AS A MATTER OF FACT *To maintain a consistent edge when using a combination of selection tools, make sure the Feather setting in the Options bar is the same each time you change tools.*

Subtract From a Selection

You can also modify a current selection by subtracting pixels from it. In our case, the initial selection we made included too much background around the stem of the dandelion, so we need to remove some pixels. Here again, we can use a different selection tool for this operation. This time, since we know that we'll be working around the stem (which is somewhat straight), we'll try the Polygonal Lasso tool.

Click the Subtract From Selection button in the Options bar now and select the Polygonal Lasso tool from the Toolbox—it's another hidden tool, like the Elliptical Marquee, so click the Lasso tool icon in the Toolbox and hold the mouse button down until you see the hidden tools, then click the Polygonal Lasso tool. Again, check the Feather and Anti-aliased settings in the Options bar for consistency with the previous parts of the selection.

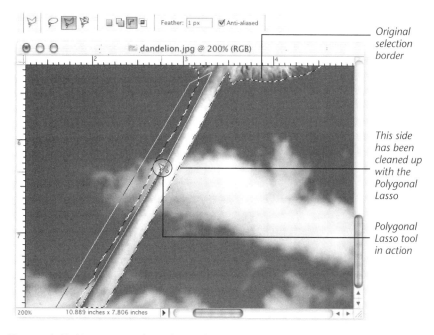

Figure 4-7 *You can use the Polygonal Lasso to remove pixels from or add pixels to an active selection.*

Before you use it, you should know that the Polygonal Lasso tool behaves differently than the regular Lasso tool. Straight-line segments are its only interest, so it's the wrong tool, for example, to make a curved or irregular selection. It works a lot like a connect-the-dots puzzle. To try it, click once to define a starting point, move the mouse, click again, move the mouse, and so on—each click tells Elements where to place the endpoints of each line segment. And a double-click tells Elements to finish the last line segment, to complete the selection for you. We did this a few times to clean up our selection border of the dandelion. And now that we have a selection we like we can do just about anything with the pixels it contains. We'll start with a simple copy and paste and make other transformations later.

Copy and Paste

We want to show you how to copy and paste a selection because it's often the very first step to image manipulation and it will clearly demonstrate why selections are a basic part of many image-editing techniques.

With your selection still active (you should see the marching ants), go to **Edit | Copy** and then to **Edit | Paste**. Although the marching ants disappear at this point, you get a nice surprise in return. If you pull the Layers palette down from the Palette Well you should see two layers in the palette: your original image and the copy you just pasted (named Layer 1). Anytime you copy and paste, Elements adds a new layer to contain the copy automatically (see Chapter 7 for a full discussion of layers), which is great because copied pixels on a layer of their own can be transformed in just about any way imaginable, without affecting the original image that's underneath. We'll show you what we mean in the next section.

Figure 4-8 Paste a copy and instantly get a new layer.

Flip, Scale, Rotate, and Move

Since no two dandelions are exactly the same, we want to make the copy of our dandelion look just a little bit different than the original. To do this we'll make some adjustments, starting with a flip.

Flip

Click the layer's name (Layer 1) in the Layers palette to make it active, which tells Elements to perform our commands on that layer only. Now go to **Image | Rotate | Flip Layer Horizontal** to flip the content of that layer. In the case of our copied dandelion, it's a good start, but still not quite different enough from the original.

> **AS A MATTER OF FACT**   *The first six commands from the **Image | Rotate** menu affect an entire file, rather than just a layer or selection.*

Scale

To further transform the copy, go to **Image | Resize | Scale**. You should now see a selection with little boxes along the border that are called *handles*. Grab a corner handle and drag to resize the copied selection. To keep the original proportions in tact as you scale, click the Maintain aspect ration button on the Options bar (see Figure 4-9) before you resize. But if proportions aren't a concern, just grab and pull any handle along the selection border and when you're pleased with the results, click the Commit icon in the Options bar.

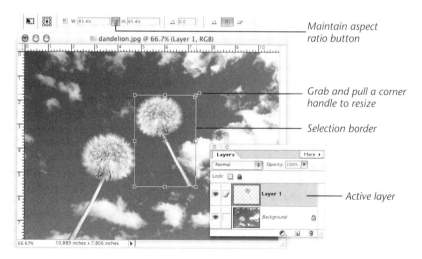

Figure 4-9   Scale a selection or a whole layer by resizing the selection border.

Rotate

We want to show you the Rotate option here because it's one more basic manipulation that's quick and easy to perform. In fact, Elements provides built-in rotations that you can apply to either selections or layers (maybe you noticed them when you used the flip command in the **Image | Rotate** menu). You can rotate 90° Left or Right, or even 180°. But since we want some freedom, we'll use the Free Rotate command:

1. Go to **Image | Rotate | Free Rotate Layer**. As with the Scale command, a selection border with handles appears.

2. Position the cursor outside the selection border until it changes into a curved double arrow, which means you can start to rotate.

3. Click and drag either clockwise or counter-clockwise.

4. Click the Commit icon in the Options bar when you're satisfied.

> **AS A MATTER OF FACT**   *The Options bar is always full of useful items, no matter what tool or function you're using. Check here often, as a habit, and investigate the various settings.*

Move

Now that we have a copy that looks different from the original, we can position it on the page to finish our image. As you might expect, the Move tool is the tool for the job, whether it's repositioning selections or layers. In this case, since the copy is on a layer of its own, we'll just move the whole layer. To do so:

1. Select the Move tool from the Toolbox.

2. Click the layer's name in the Layers palette to activate it.

3. Position the Move tool's cursor inside the selection border.

4. Click and drag the layer to its new position.

5. To deactivate the Move tool, simply select any other tool from the Toolbox.

Selection border

Move tool's cursor

Figure 4-10 *Use the Move tool to reposition the layer that contains the copy.*

Make a Complex Selection

As you learned, the Lasso tool is a good choice when you need to make a selection that's irregular in shape. But it requires a steady hand and a good deal of patience. Use it to select a complex shape and you'll be signing up for some very tedious work, indeed.

One possible solution to the tedium is the Magnetic Lasso tool. Although it's a relative of the Lasso, the similarities don't go deep. Where the Lasso is a simple tool that works intuitively, the Magnetic Lasso is a complex one that takes some getting used to. But the time it'll take to master its quirks will be time well-spent. To that end, we'll show you a few things to get you started with the Magnetic Lasso, then you can explore it further on your own.

In our example, we want to copy a parrot from one image and paste it into another image. We could use the Lasso tool, but, as we mentioned, that could get tedious. We could try the Magic Wand, but it's unpredictable and works best under very narrow circumstances: lots of contrast and little variation in tonal values. There is the Selection Brush tool, which is great for people who are more comfortable with brushes, but it can be difficult to get into tight corners.

Since our parrot happens to be part of a relatively simple image—he is mostly isolated from surroundings that are blurry and similarly colored—the conditions are right for the Magnetic Lasso tool. This selection tool is suited to situations when you want to make a quick selection of an irregular shape that stands out from its background. But as is the case with many tools, we first need to set the tool options to control its behavior.

Set Options

The Magnetic Lasso tool is hidden behind the Lasso tool in the Toolbox. So to select it, click and hold the mouse button down over the Lasso tool icon to reveal the hidden tool choices, then click the Polygonal Lasso tool. Now look at the Options bar. You know by now that the options that appear in this bar change depending on what tool or command is in use. See how the options available to the Magnetic Lasso tool are different than the ones we set for the Lasso tool? To get you started, here's a rundown of the various Magnetic Lasso Options bar settings.

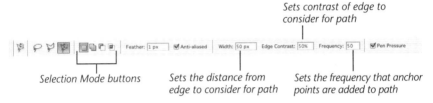

Figure 4-11 *Control the Magnetic Lasso with the Options bar settings.*

Selection Mode

The Selection mode buttons appear in the left-hand portion of the Options bar (see Figure 4-11): New Selection, Add To Selection, Subtract From Selection, Intersect with a selection. We've already used most of these buttons, so you may have guessed which is the right choice in this case: Click the New Selection button now.

Feather and Anti-aliased

Make sure the Anti-aliased setting is enabled and enter a Feather setting of 1 or 2. As you learned earlier in this chapter, these settings control the appearance of a selection edge; the Feather setting controls the softness of an edge, and the Anti-aliased option helps prevent jagged edges.

Width, Edge Contrast, and Frequency

You may see the settings we just talked about in the Options bar when other tools are in use, since they are common to a few selection tools. But the rest of the settings you see control the tools behavior, so they are unique to the Magnetic Lasso tool.

You see, the Magnetic Lasso tool is supposed to do all the hard work when you trace along the edge of an object to select it. But it's best used in high-contrast situations when the object you want to select has well-defined edges. So if the conditions are right, the Magnetic Lasso's selection is automatically drawn (like a magnet) to the edges of an object—if everything works properly. To stack the odds in your favor, you can use the following guidelines to play with the settings in the Options bar.

Width   The Width setting corresponds to an area of edge detection. You can think of it as a sort of fudge factor. The higher the number here, the less fussy you have to be with the tool's cursor as you drag along the edge of an object. So the higher the number in the Width field, the more magnetic pull the object's edges have on the tool's cursor. However, this works well only on images that are high contrast and contain clean edges. Our parrot image is average in this respect, so we started with a value of 50 for the Options bar Width setting.

Edge Contrast   The Edge Contrast setting works in a similar fashion to the Width setting. For edges that contrast sharply from their surroundings, you can use a high number here and be a little less conscientious when making a selection. As with the Width setting, the lower the number, the more careful you have to be when tracing the edges of an object to get a good result. We used 50 for this setting as well.

Frequency   To specify how often the tool puts down anchor points along the selection border, use the Frequency setting. The higher the number, the more anchor points you'll get, which is useful in especially complex selections since more anchor points usually means more detail. We like to use a setting of about 50 or so for general use, but you can go as high as 100.

It may seem like a lot to consider before putting the Magnetic Lasso to work, but you can boil it all down to this: If you have a crisp image and good definition between the edge you want to select and its surroundings, use higher settings in the Width and Edge Contrast fields of the Options bar; but if the object's edges are less defined from their surroundings, use smaller numbers and stay close to the edge when you trace.

Use the Magnetic Lasso

Once you've addressed the Options bar, you can put the Magnetic Lasso to use. To start, position the cursor at a starting point along the edge of an object, then click once and drag—you don't have to hold down the mouse button as you drag. Just drag the mouse along the edge of an object and watch the selection border snap to the strongest edges of an object. Although it may seem like magic, you shouldn't expect perfection from this tool, since it's mainly built for speed, not accuracy. The truth is, an almost perfect selection is often good enough and, as you know, you can always modify a selection later to clean it up.

Figure 4-12
The beginnings of our selection look promising.

Although the Options bar settings should keep the behavior of the Magnetic lasso in-check (if set properly), you can control a selection edge manually, if needed. Let's say the tool's selection doesn't snap to the edge of an object in a particular area—in our case, the lasso refused to include the tip of the parrot's beak in the selection. We had to force our selection to that part of the parrot's beak by clicking the mouse button along the edge to add anchor points manually.

AS A MATTER OF FACT *If you don't like a segment of the selection made with the Magnetic Lasso, press DELETE to erase segments one at a time, starting with the most recent. Delete all the segments if you want to start over, or press CMD + PERIOD (Mac) or CTRL + PERIOD (Windows) to cancel the selection in progress.*

You'll find that the Magnetic Lasso tool is like the other lassos in that you have to close or finish a selection. To do so, drag back to the point where you started the selection and when you see a little circle appear on the cursor, click. If it's not perfect, don't worry. You can use any selection tool you like to add and subtract from these selections, as you did earlier in this chapter. Or you can try the additional tips and tricks that follow.

> **AS A MATTER OF FACT**   *If you spent a lot of time perfecting a selection, you can save it for use later on. With a selection active, go to* **Select | Save Selection**, *choose* **New** *from the Selection pop-up menu, name it, and click OK. To use that saved selection, go to* **Select | Load Selection**.

Modify a Selection

You already know how to add to or subtract from a current selection, so we want to show you some additional ways to modify a selection through menu commands. In our case, the selection of the parrot isn't quite right yet. When we zoom in to take a better look, we see that the Magnetic Lasso missed a few pixels all the way around the parrot, so the selection border is just inside the edge of the parrot.

To include or subtract pixels from the perimeter of a selection, a number of menu commands help, although each lends itself to particular situations. We used the Grow command to adjust our parrot selection, but you can consult the following sections to see which best suits your needs.

Grow

To add adjacent areas of similar color to a current selection, you can try the Grow command, but because the command borrows the Tolerance setting from the Magic Wand tool, you first have to click the Magic Wand icon in the Toolbox.

Now check the Tolerance setting in the Options bar. The higher the Tolerance setting, the broader the range of colors that will be added to the selection. So when the Grow command looks here for instructions, it finds how little or how much to add to the current selection. In our case, we needed just a little bit added to our selection of the parrot, so we set the Magic Wand Tolerance to 30 (which is relatively low), then went to **Select | Grow**. If it includes too much, click the Step Backward button in the Shortcuts bar, reset the Magic Wand's Tolerance setting to a lower value, then try the Grow command again.

Original selection border   After the Grow and Smooth commands

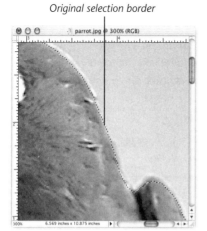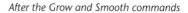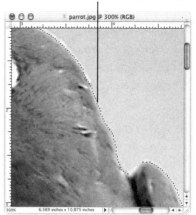

Figure 4-13 *We used the Grow and Smooth commands to expand and smooth our selection border.*

Similar

But the Grow command adds only pixels that are *adjacent* to the current selection border, so if you want to add pixels of a similar color from *all over* the image, go to **Select | Similar**. This command also looks to the Magic Wand's Tolerance setting for guidance, so the higher the number here, the more pixels will be included. The difference with the Similar command is that pixels from all over the image will be included, as long as they fall within the tolerance range.

Expand or Contract

If you just want to nudge a selection edge a pixel or two in either direction—without regard for color or tolerance settings—go to **Select | Modify | Expand** or **Select | Modify | Contract**. In either case, enter a value (up to 16 pixels) in the box that pops up and click OK. The selection border will move in or out by the number of pixels you specified.

Smooth

And if your selection border just needs the rough edges smoothed, try the Smooth command to clean up stray pixels that fall inside or outside the selection border. Go to **Select | Modify | Smooth** and enter a value between 1 and 100 in the box that pops up to control how far Elements will search, on either side of the current selection border, for stray pixels. We used a value of 3, which smoothed our selection nicely (see Figure 4-13).

We could go on and on about modifying and perfecting a selection border, but then we'd never get to the fun stuff. You could spend hours refining a selection, but chances are, no one will notice if your edges aren't perfect. What's most important is that you know how to make basic selections so you can then transform and manipulate them in any way you choose.

Incorporate a Copy

You may remember that our objective was to copy the parrot and paste it into another picture. So that's just what we did. It's just like the copy and paste we performed on our dandelion image, only this time, we pasted the copy into a new image. And as with the dandelion image, we end up with a layer that contains the copy, which can be flipped, scaled, rotated, or repositioned. But we want to show you a few tricks to successfully incorporate a copied selection into another image with seamless and convincing results.

Make It Seamless

It's likely that any flaws in your selection will become apparent once your copy is pasted onto a new background. For instance, we can see a faint halo of white around our parrot (see Figure 4-14) because he's now on a different color. It's a common problem, but as long as the copy is on its own layer, there's a quick way to clean it up.

Remove a Halo

To remove the halo of pixels that often plagues copied selections:

1. In the Layers palette, click the name of the layer that contains the copy, then select the Magic Wand tool from the Toolbox.

2. In the Options bar, set the Tolerance to 100 and make sure the Use All Layers option is turned off (unchecked).

3. Position the Magic Wand outside the boundary of copied pixels and click once—the Wand should select everything *but* the copied pixels.

4. Go to **Select | Modify | Expand** and enter a value of 1 or 2 pixels.

5. Go to **Select | Feather**, enter a value of 2 to 3 pixels.

6. Press **DELETE** one or two times—or as many times as it takes to make the halo disappear.

Figure 4-14

When a copy and paste is performed, halos may appear.

The halo effect

dishes.jpg @ 100% (Layer 1, RGB)

100%   13.917 inches x 9.153 inches

Make it Convincing

After we cleaned up the halo on our parrot, we reduced it in size, flipped it, then positioned it with the Move tool. But to make the incorporation more convincing, we need to make a few more selections. If you look at Figure 4-16 you'll see how it looks like the parrot's tail is behind the satellite dish on which it's perched. That's what we mean when we say convincing. To achieve this, we had to select and delete parts of its tail to create this illusion.

Since we want the tail to look like it's behind the top of the satellite dish, we want to remove only the part of the parrot that overlaps the satellite dish. No more and no less. To be convincing, it should match up exactly with the edge of the dish. So instead of selecting parts of the parrot, we'll use the Magic Wand tool to select the areas that surround the dish. It sounds counter-intuitive, but trust us on this.

Use the Magic Wand

First we chose the Magic Wand tool from the Toolbox and clicked the New Selection button in the Options bar, entered a value of 70 for the Tolerance, activated both the Anti-aliased and Contiguous options, and turned the Use All Layers option off, as seen in Figure 4-15.

Now we can click the target layer's name (Background) in the Layers Palette, position the cursor on the part of the image we want to select (the sky that surrounds the satellite dish), and click once with the Magic Wand tool.

Options bar settings for Magic Wand tool

Layer that contains copy

Target layer

Figure 4-15   *A selection border indicates what the Magic Wand selected.*

Select the Inverse

You might be wondering why we selected sky, when our interest really lies in the top of the satellite dish that our parrot sits atop. There's a good reason that reveals a nifty trick. In our case, it was easier to select the sky with the Magic Wand than it would have been to select the satellite dish with any of the lasso tools. So we just took the path of least resistance. Then go to **Select | Inverse** to tell Elements to select the opposite of what's currently selected.

Now we have a selection that includes the top of the satellite dish, which is good. But it also includes the parrot's claws, which isn't what we want. So we used the Lasso tool to subtract the claws from the selection. Then, to delete the parrot's tail, we click the name of the parrot's layer in the Layer Palette and press **DELETE**. And now it looks like the tail is hidden behind the top of the satellite dish (see Figure 4-16).

Figure 4-16 *A completely convincing incorporation*

We urge you to explore the selection tools further to build on the basics we showed you. While you may not run across the specific examples we discuss in this chapter, like a parrot or a dandelion, you know how to isolate areas of an image so you can copy and paste, or even scale and rotate them. But while these techniques are important, there's a lot more to discover. As we've mentioned, selecting pixels is only the first step to image manipulation. With practice and a little confidence, you'll learn that you can combine the concepts you just learned with those covered in other chapters of this book to create stunning images.

Add Type

Sure, Photoshop Elements delivers powerful image-editing capabilities to the masses. No doubt this software can do some amazing things. We admit that the ability to combine digital images is appealing; that the desire to slap a human head on the family pooch might be irresistible. And the capability to transform a modern color snapshot into an aged sepia-toned treasure with the click of a mouse is seductive. By all means, flex those image-editing muscles. But don't forget the possibilities of type, for goodness sake.

Add captions and cartoon bubbles to photos; create eye-catching headlines for a brochure or charts and graphs for a newsletter; make buttons and banners for a web site; combine text and images to create a collage, your own stationery, or flash cards; you can even design a logo. To add a little something extra to an image, try type.

Don't be fooled, though. Although there are similarities, Elements is not a word-processing program. There's no spell check (so have a dictionary handy), and there aren't options to indent text or control line and paragraph spacing. Elements is built to handle small bits and snippets of text for display purposes, such as headlines and captions, not paragraphs of text. So save your newsletter or brochure copy for a word-processing program, and use Elements to create stunning headlines and eye-catching graphics.

Create Type

Say, for instance, you want to add type to a photo to transform it from an OK snapshot into a hilarious postcard. It's as simple as adding type in a word-processing program: enter type, change the size and color of the type, and add or delete characters as needed. But Elements allows you to do much more. In the following sections, we'll show you the basic concepts and tools of adding words to an image.

Enter Type

First, open an image and pull the Layers palette down from the Palette Well, so both it and your Image Window are visible. Select the Horizontal Type tool (the "T" button) from the Toolbox. Notice how the information on the Options bar changes—we'll talk about these options in the Format section a little later. Click anywhere on the Image Area to show Elements where you want to begin typing. The blinking I-beam indicates that your Type tool is ready to go. You should know that Elements will continue to add characters even if it runs past the edge of the image, so press **ENTER** (Windows) or **RETURN** (Mac) to tell Elements when you want to start a new line of text.

Don't worry about how the text looks or its position on the image yet. For now, just begin typing, and when you're done, click the Commit button (the check mark) in the Options bar (see Figure 5-3). It's like saying to Elements: OK, I like this type and want to keep it around for a while. To oblige, Elements gives your type a layer of its own and names the layer for you. For instance, if you type the words "Wish you were here" (see Figure 5-1), and commit to it as we did, Elements creates a type layer named "Wish you were here."

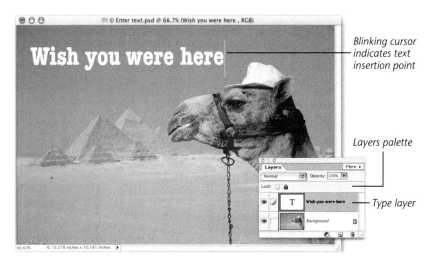

Blinking cursor indicates text insertion point

Layers palette

Type layer

Figure 5-1 *Use the Type tool to enter text.*

Take a peek at your Layers palette now to see how Elements added a type layer. You should see your image on the bottom layer, and the type layer you just created on top (see Figure 5-1). See the "T" in the thumbnail in the Layers palette? That "T" indicates that the layer is a type layer. To find out more about layers, refer to Chapter 7.

Edit

Type layers are great because they let you move, edit, and embellish text without affecting other areas of an image. It's as if the text were floating on top of the image. To show you what me mean, let's edit the text we just created.

Select the Type tool (if it's not already) and click anywhere on the text you created in the last exercise. A blinking I-beam indicates the insertion point. If the insertion point is not where you want it, either click a new spot on the text or use the arrow keys on your keyboard to move it. From the insertion point, you can drag the cursor to select one or more characters; double-click to select a whole word, triple-click to select a whole line, or choose **Select | All** to select all of the text. These text selection techniques should be your first step when changing things like the font, size, color, or alignment of individual characters in your text. And they are always required when you want to delete, copy, cut, or replace any or all of your text.

AS A MATTER OF FACT   *Double-click the type layer's "T" button in the Layers palette thumbnail to select the entire contents of that type layer.*

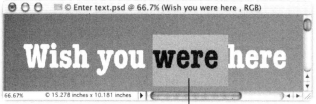

Figure 5-2
Make a selection with the Type tool to edit.

A selection made with the Type tool

Format

When you format type, you change its appearance. If you want to change the appearance of only *some* of the text, you need to make a selection with the Type tool first. But if you want to format *all* of the text on a type layer, you can do so without making any selections. To format all the type on a layer, click the type layer in the Layers palette to make sure it is active. If you see the blinking cursor on the text, select any other tool from the Toolbox and then select the Type tool again, but don't click the text. Now you're ready to format the text.

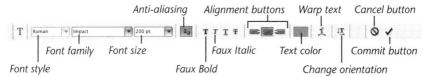

Figure 5-3 *The Options bar when the Type tool is active*

Change the Font

To change the typeface or *font* of the text, choose a font family from the Font Family pop-up menu in the Options bar. Then, choose a font style from the Font Style pop-up menu in the Options bar. These font style options vary—some font families, for instance, don't offer a Bold option in the Font Style menu. In such a case, you could click the Faux Bold button (see Figure 5-3) in the Options bar, but you'd first have to select the type—the Faux Bold, Faux Italic, Underline, and Strikethrough options are available only to type that's been selected with the Type tool first.

> **AS A MATTER OF FACT**   *To select all characters on a type layer with the Type tool, click the text to get the blinking cursor, then go to **Select | All**.*

Resize

To make your text larger or smaller, choose a point size from the font size pop-up menu (see Figure 5-3). Points are a standard unit of measurement for type. All you need to know is that the larger the number, the larger your text. You can type a value directly into this field if you like, but if you're unfamiliar with point sizes, start with the pop-up menu until you get a feel for what's big and what's way too big.

> **AS A MATTER OF FACT**   *Although points are the standard unit of measurement when it comes to type, you can change this default to pixels or millimeters. Go to **Edit | Preferences | Units & Rulers** (Mac OS 9.x, Windows) or **Photoshop Elements | Preferences | Units & Rulers** (Mac OS X).*

Anti-Alias

When you create type in Elements, the default enables the Anti-aliasing option, which is good because you want it on at all times. Without it, your type will have ragged edges. To demonstrate, select the Type tool, click the name of the type layer in the Layers palette, and zoom in on your text until you can see tiny jagged edges along the curves of a letter. Don't be alarmed. These jaggies are normal and inevitable. Besides, they won't be noticeable when the image is viewed at its actual size or when you print it—these aren't the ragged edges we mentioned. Now, click the Anti-aliasing button in the Options bar (see Figure 5-3) to turn it off and watch those jagged edges get worse. Click the Anti-aliasing button again to turn it back on.

> **AS A MATTER OF FACT** *If Anti-aliasing doesn't fix jagged type, you might have a font problem—try a different font. If it's still jagged, the problem could be caused by low resolution—see Chapter 2 for a discussion of resolution. And if this still doesn't fix the problem, the font may be installed incorrectly or corrupted.*

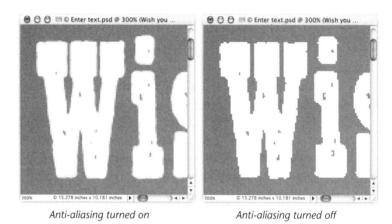

Anti-aliasing turned on   Anti-aliasing turned off

Figure 5-4   *Keep Anti-aliasing turned on for smooth type.*

Align

The alignment buttons in the Options bar (Figure 5-3) work like they do in a word-processing program. Each option aligns your text relative to the place you first clicked to enter the text. Their names say it all: Left Align, Center Align, and Right Align.

To experiment with alignment, you'll need a couple lines of text: Select the Type tool and click your text just after the last character; press **RETURN** (Mac) or **ENTER** (Windows) to move the cursor to the next line and type more text. Now you can try each of the alignment buttons on the Options bar—there's no need to click the type or select it, as long as the Type tool is active.

> **AS A MATTER OF FACT** *If your text is vertically oriented (as most text is), the alignment buttons available on the Options bar change to Top Align, Center Align, and Bottom Align.*

Pick a Color

Click the Text Color box in the Options bar (see Figure 5-3) to pick a color for your type. Or click the Foreground Color box at the bottom of the Toolbox. Either way, Elements will open the Color Picker. Choose a color that you like and click OK (for help with the Color Picker, see Chapter 6).

As mentioned at the beginning of this section, you *can* apply formatting to individual characters on a type layer if you like. Say you want just one word in your text to be a different color than the rest. You first have to make a selection with the Type tool, so Elements knows which parts of the text you want to change. You make the selection first and *then* click the Text Color box to open the Color Picker.

Change Orientation

As you probably discovered by now, Elements provides two tools for entering type: the Horizontal Type tool and the Vertical Type tool (they share the same spot in the Toolbox). The Horizontal Type tool is best for most general use. You can always change the orientation of your text after you type it in (we'll show you how in a minute). In either case, orientation affects the entire contents of a type layer. So if you want one line of text horizontal and another vertical, you have to create two separate type layers, each with its own orientation. To change the orientation of text:

1. Place the Type tool's cursor anywhere on the text in your file. Or just click the type layer in the Layers palette and select the Type tool.

2. Click the Change Text Orientation button in the Options bar (see Figure 5-3). The orientation of all text is changed.

3. Click the button again to change it back.

Move It

We covered all the basics but one up to this point: positioning or moving your text. The Move tool works the same on a Type layer as it does on any layer. Click the type layer in the Layers palette and select the Move tool from the Toolbox. You should see a selection border (a dotted line and squares) surrounding your text. Move the cursor to a place inside the selection border, then click and drag the text to its new position. Or instead of dragging the layer, you could use the arrows on your keyboard to make incremental movements.

Those are the basics of adding type to your images. You can make text bigger, change the color, or even move it. While this might satisfy all your type needs, Elements can do a lot more. The rest of this chapter will show you how to add a little something extra to your type; we're pretty sure you'll be impressed by the results.

Figure 5-5
Move type layers with the Move tool.

Click, hold, and drag with the Move tool   Selection border

Warp

With the basics of formatting out of the way, we can get down to some more unusual type treatments. A lot of programs can add basic text to an image, but what sets Elements apart is how easily it transforms boring letters into just about anything you can dream up. In fact, Elements offers a feature called the text Warp that is dedicated to these transformations. We'll show you how to use the text Warp, as well as some other tricks to spice up your type. And although some techniques seem more complex than others, the underlying principles are the same in each case: First you enter text with the Type tool, then you format it; where you go from there depends on your desired end result. Try our suggestions first to get acquainted with the general techniques, then explore on your own.

Make Waves

Say you want to make text look like it's floating on water. To do this, we'll use an image of water under our text to enhance the effect, and the text Warp feature in the Options bar. You can use the text you created earlier in the chapter to follow along. Like orientation and alignment, a text warp affects the entire type layer and can't be applied to individual characters. Since this is the case, there's no need to drag and select characters with the Type tool; just click the type layer in the Layers palette, select the Type tool, and click the Warp button in the Options bar. The box that opens is where you control the particulars of a warp.

Click the Warp
Style menu, then
choose a style

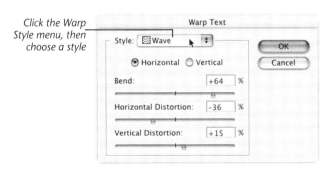

Figure 5-6
Control the behavior of a warp from the Warp Text box.

Click the Style pop-up menu at the top of the box to see the available warp options. Since we're going for the water effect, we'll choose Wave. The Horizontal and Vertical radio buttons here affect the orientation of the warp. For most warps, Horizontal is best. That's really all you have to know to set up a text warp. You don't have to touch another setting if you don't want to. But those other settings offer a great deal of control and flexibility (literally, in this case), so we want to investigate them a bit.

AS A MATTER OF FACT *If your text contains a Faux Bold style, you won't be able to perform text warps. Select your text and click the appropriate button in the Options bar to remove the faux style, then click the Warp button.*

The Bend value corresponds to the amount of distortion in the warp; we set ours to +64. The Horizontal and Vertical Distortion settings affect the perspective of the warp. We set our Horizontal Distortion to –36 and the Vertical to +15, but you can experiment with yours. Fortunately, you can watch the changes occur in real time as you change these settings, so you don't have to guess. When you like what you see, click OK.

Indicates a warp is in use

Figure 5-7 *A Wave warp, with the Overlay blending mode applied to the type layer*

Perhaps the best thing about text warps is that the type layer remains editable with the Type tool, even after you apply a warp. Try it now—select the Type tool and edit your text. And if you ever want to remove a warp, simply click the Warp button in the Options bar and select None from the Style pop-up menu in the Warp Text box. You can even change the formatting of your text, like the font, size, or color while a warp is in use. Or you can set the type layer's blending mode to something like Overlay, as we did with ours, to blend the type with the image on the layer below it (see Chapter 7 for more about blending modes).

Transform

But text warps aren't the last word on text distortion. You can also try some commands found in the Menu bar at the top of the screen. Select **Image | Transform** from the Menu bar to see these options: Free Transform, Skew, Distort, and Perspective. Each of these does something different and while we can't cover them all here, we'll show you two of them so you can see how they work.

First, you should notice that two of the four options here are grayed out: Distort and Perspective. That's because, as long as your text is a type layer—which means it's editable with the Type tool—these options are not available. You first have to simplify the type layer, which we'll show you in the next section. But we'll try the Skew command first, since it doesn't require a simplified type layer.

Skew

While we could skew a type layer that has a warp applied to it, we'd rather show you the Skew command on its own so you can see what it does. To follow along, first remove the text warp you applied in the previous section:

1. Click the Warp button in the Options bar and choose None from the Style menu, then click OK.

2. With the type layer still active, go to **Image | Transform | Skew**.

3. What you see surrounding your text is a selection border. Grab one of the little boxes (handles) in a corner of the selection border and drag up, down, left, or right.

4. Let go of your mouse button when you like the changes you've made.

5. Click the Commit button (check mark) in the Options bar to accept the change.

We had you accept the change so we can show you something really great. You can apply the Free Transform and Skew commands and still go back and edit your text. Try that now: Select one word of your text and type something else to change it. Over time you'll find this ability to edit text, even after you've altered its appearance, a great advantage.

> **AS A MATTER OF FACT** *You can also continue to edit text with the Type tool after applying Rotate and Scale commands (found under the Image menu).*

Figure 5-8
*Even after you
skew text, the type
layer is still editable
with the Type tool.*

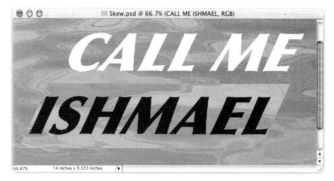

Change Perspective

There are some things that you just can't do with a type layer. For instance, you can't apply a Filter or paint on a type layer. And, as we mentioned, you can't use the Distort or Perspective commands. (Remember how they were grayed out when you went to **Image | Transform**?) To do these things with type, you first have to *simplify* the type layer—this converts an editable type layer into a regular image layer. More precisely, it converts vector information into to bitmap information (see Chapter 2 for more on vector and bitmap images). And while simplifying a type layer makes editing with the Type tool impossible—no more quick changes to the spelling or formatting—it allows the use of the Brush tool, filters, and the Eraser.

One command that requires a simplified layer is the Perspective command we mentioned earlier. We'll try it, but first use the Step Backward button on the Shortcuts bar to undo the skew you applied in the previous section. To simplify the layer and then transform it:

1. Click the type layer in the Layers palette and go to **Layer | Simplify Layer**. That's it; your type layer is now simplified.

2. Notice how the thumbnail in the Layers palette changed for the type layer—it's no longer a big "T"—now it's a regular layer with a regular layer's thumbnail.

3. Now you can use the Perspective command: Go to **Image | Transform | Perspective**.

4. You should see a selection border with little square handles; grab a handle and drag in any direction to see what happens.

5. Click the Cancel or Commit button to either deny or accept the changes you see in the Image Window.

Figure 5-9 *Our transformed type layer*

Add Depth

As you just learned, you can enhance your text in many ways (warps and some transformations) without giving up the editability of type layers. If you're fickle like us, these options are preferable. Or maybe you're a designer who makes frequent changes to text, based on the whims of a client. In any case, we'll show you some quick and tidy ways to add shine to type while still being able to edit type layers.

We use the Layer Styles in the following examples because we like their flexibility and ease of use—and because there's no quicker way to get great results with type.

Bevels

We'll start with one of the most useful, the Emboss Layer Style. It creates beveled edges or an embossed effect with both type and objects. And it's really easy to use:

1. Click the type layer in the Layers palette to make it active.

2. Pull the Layer Styles palette down from the Palette Well.

3. Select Bevels from the pop-up menu in the Layer Styles palette.

4. Select any embossed style from the options available in the palette; we chose Simple Inner.

Shadows

To show you how to combine Layer Styles, we'll add a shadow to our beveled type. Select Drop Shadows from the pop-up menu in the Layer Styles palette and then select any shadow style you like (we chose the Soft Edge drop shadow).

To refine the effect, double-click the little circle button to the right of the layer's name in the Layers palette (it looks like an italic "f" in a black circle) to open the Style Settings box. This is where you alter and control a Layer Style (see Chapter 8 for a discussion of Layer styles and the Style Settings box).

Grab the Shadow Distance slider and drag it to the right to move the shadow away from the type for a more dramatic effect. With the Preview option turned on, you can watch changes occur to your text, as you alter the style settings—so watch the Image Window, stop when you see something you like, then click OK.

Figure 5-10   *Fine-tune a Layer Style's behavior in the Style Settings box.*

Plastic

Before we continue, you should know that if you click the Clear Style button in the top right of the Layer Styles palette you remove all Layer Styles from a layer. Do this now to clear the bevel and drop shadow effects from your type layer.

For a real kick, try any of the Wow Plastic Layer Styles. Select Wow Plastic from the pop-up menu in the Layer Styles palette and then choose any option you like. These particular styles really shine when they are applied to a layer that's on top of something else, like an image or another color. Why? Because they make your type look as if it's made of translucent plastic, so you can see through it.

Fill Text

As we just showed you, Layer Styles are easy to use with type. But if you want to take your text to the next level, you can fill it with an image or a pattern. It's almost as easy as the Layer Styles and the results look so professional that you'll want to use these techniques again and again.

Rusted Metal

To get a fresh start, go to **File | New** to begin a new file, make it any size you like, select RGB from the Mode menu, and click the White radio button in the Contents section of the New box, then click OK. Now create a type layer using the techniques we showed you at the beginning of the chapter: Format your type and warp it if you want, but there's no need to pick a color, since the text will be filled with the texture you create:

1. Pull the Effects palette down from the Palette Well and find the Textures library in the pop-up menu (upper-left corner) in the Effects palette.

2. Select the Rusted Metal option and click the Apply button (upper-right of the Effects palette). These Texture effects create a new layer for you automatically—in fact, some textures (like Pine) create two or more layers.

3. Look at the Layers palette to see the three layers: the white Background layer, a type layer, and a layer that contains the rusted metal texture.

4. Click the type layer to make it active and link the texture layer to it—click the box to the right of the texture layer's eye button in the Layers palette (for more about linking, see Chapter 7).

5. Make sure the type layer is below the texture layer(s). Then go to **Layer | Group Linked**.

When you group layers as you did in that last step, the bottom layer becomes the *base layer* for the group, which means all layers in the group take on the shape of the base layer. So you can use this same technique to fill text with a photo instead of a texture: Just replace the texture layer with an image layer, make sure it's above the type layer, and then group them. For a better understanding of layers and grouping, see Chapter 7.

To make this effect more stunning, click the type layer in the Layers palette, choose the Inner Shadow library from the Layer Style palette pop-up menu, and choose an option. We chose High for our inner shadow. You're starting to see how you can combine Effects and Layer Styles—you could even warp the text if you like—to really stretch the impact of type.

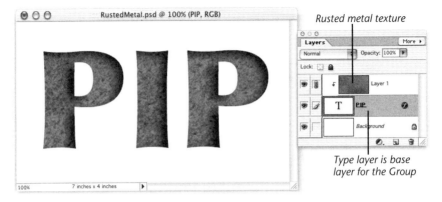

Rusted metal texture

Type layer is base layer for the Group

Figure 5-11 *Group layers to fill type with a texture or image.*

> **AS A MATTER OF FACT** *Even after grouping and applying Layer Styles to the type layer, it can still be edited with the Type tool.*

Easy Patterns

If you're not picky about what fills your text—you just want something, anything to fill it—the Patterns library in the Layer Styles palette is great. It's quick and easy. The results aren't as stunning, but they get the job done. Again, a huge selling point to this approach (in addition to its speed) is that the type remains editable with the Type tool. So it's a great one to use if you know you might want to edit the text down the road.

Create a type layer, click it in the Layers palette to make sure it's active, and then select a pattern from the Patterns library on the Layer Styles palette. That's it. Of course, you can always add some more Layer Styles to the mix, like a drop shadow or a glow, to further enhance the type.

Rusted Metal Revisited

The last example of filled text we want to show you is a little different. This time, we'll use the *Type Mask tool*. As with the regular Type tool, there's a horizontal and vertical version of the Type Mask tool. For now, select the Horizontal Type Mask tool from the Toolbox—it shares a spot with the regular Type tool. Click the Type tool button and hold down the mouse button, then click the Horizontal Type Mask tool (it's the "T" with a dashed outline) to select it.

The Type Mask tool is made for just this kind of effect and little else. The biggest difference between the regular Type tool and the Type Mask tool is that text created with the Type Mask tool is *never* editable with the regular Type tool. It just creates a selection border in the shapes of letters or words (for more on selections, see Chapter 4). A demonstration of the tool and difference between it and the regular Type tool follows.

1. Start a new file, as you did at the beginning of the Rusted Metal section of this chapter.

2. Click the New Layer button at the bottom of the Layers palette (to the left of the Trash button).

3. Select the Horizontal Type Mask tool from the Toolbox, and type some text—don't be alarmed by the pink color that fills the Image Area, it's just an indication that the Type Mask tool is in action.

4. Go ahead and format the text—you can even warp it, if you like.

5. If you like the way the selection looks—the formatting—choose the Rusted Metal option from the Textures library in the Effects palette and click the Apply button. Your type selection should now be filled with the texture you chose.

6. Go to **Selection | Deselect**.

AS A MATTER OF FACT The Type Mask tool does not add a new layer to a file automatically, like the regular Type tool does. Remember to add a new layer to your file before you use the Type Mask tool, or your text will be fused to the currently active layer.

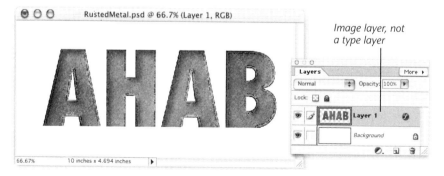

Image layer, not a type layer

Figure 5-12 *Our finished type effect*

Remember when we created a layer of texture and then grouped it with a type layer? It achieved the same thing we just did with the Type Mask tool, only it took a few more steps. While the end result looks the same, there's one difference we think important to emphasize: The rusted metal we created the first time with the Type tool is editable, but the one created with the Type Mask tool is not. While the first option may take a bit more time (not much), the benefit gained is immeasurable.

Paint

It's probably safe to bet that you'll mostly use Elements for editing existing images, like digital photos and scans. But you should know that Elements can also create electronic drawings and paintings that stand up on their own. If you want to produce your own images from scratch—whether complex masterpieces or simple shapes and drawings—Elements offers plenty of tools for the job. In fact, there are tools that practically do the painting and drawing for you, so you don't have to be an artist. Whether you're an inspired painter or doodler, there's something in this chapter for you.

We'll start with the Brush tool and some basic techniques to create a simple landscape painting. Then we'll move on to some more complex techniques, to create depth and interest in your paintings. And finally, we'll cover the fundamentals of combining paints with photos. With a few fundamentals under your belt, and a little extra practice and imagination, you should be well on your way to masterworks of your own.

Collect Materials

Any artist will tell you that even divine inspiration benefits from a little preparation. That preparation would almost certainly entail heading off to the store for an assortment of paints and brushes, stretching some canvases, and making sure you have ample light and a little elbowroom. With Elements the prep work is minimal. There are plenty of other advantages too: The materials like paint and brushes are built into the software, so there's no expense; no mess to clean up; and you don't need much room at all because Elements is your paint box, your canvas, and your easel—all in one tidy little package. If you've already launched the program, the supplies are at your fingertips, so it's just a matter of organizing the work area and preparing a canvas.

Start a Blank Canvas

If rabbit guts, stretchers, and staples sound scary to you, you're in luck. Preparing a blank canvas in Elements is painless, odorless, and quick. Although you can use a colored canvas, the painterly tradition is white, so that's what we'll do:

1. Go to **File | New** and name the file.

2. Make a selection from the Preset Sizes menu or enter values in the Width and Height fields. We made our file 5-by-3 inches.

3. Specify a Resolution of 300 pixels per inch, which should give good results from a color ink-jet printer even if we want to enlarge its printed size a bit.

4. Choose RGB Color from the Mode menu, and select the White radio button from the Contents section of the dialog box.

5. Click OK.

Figure 6-1
Set up a blank canvas from the New dialog box.

That's it. All you have to do is have a plan each time you start a canvas. Know the end use and plan the resolution and size accordingly. If you need help with this, refer to Chapter 2 for a discussion of size and resolution considerations.

Color Palette

The canvas part of our prep work was painless; but the real work starts here, with organizing and choosing our paint. Sure, we could jump right in and lay paint to canvas, grabbing colors as we go. But imagine a studio stocked with hundreds of tubes of paint, all neatly organized by color and lined up in rows; wouldn't that be nice. That's what Elements offers; all you have to do is guide it.

Foreground/Background

Choosing a color of paint in Elements is almost as easy as dipping a brush in a bucket; it is a little different, though. Say you want to paint something red. To use red paint in Elements, you must first specify red as the *foreground color*. That's because tools like the Paintbrush, Paint Bucket, and Pencil always use the *foreground color*. The default *foreground color* is always black, so if you want to paint or draw with any other color, you have to pick a new *foreground color*.

Take a look at the bottom section of the Toolbox (see Figure 6-2). Those two overlapping swatches of color show what colors are specified as the *foreground* (top) and *background* (bottom) color. You should see black and white now because these are the default colors. To change either one, click the appropriate swatch in the Toolbox to open the Color Picker.

> **AS A MATTER OF FACT** *To reset the foreground and background colors, click the Default Colors icon at the bottom of the Toolbox (see Figure 6-2). To switch the background and foreground colors, click the Switch Colors icon (curved arrow).*

Color Picker

When the Color Picker opens, the first thing you probably see is the *Color field*; it's the large box on the left that's filled with colors (see Figure 6-2). Click anywhere in the field to pick a color, but notice how the field shows only variations, from light to dark, of one color or hue. So what if you want blue, but there's no blue in the color field to choose? The triangles on either side of the *color slider* (see Figure 6-2) indicate which color (from the entire spectrum) is active in the color field. Click anywhere on the color slider to set a new reference point; the triangles move to indicate the new reference point on the color slider.

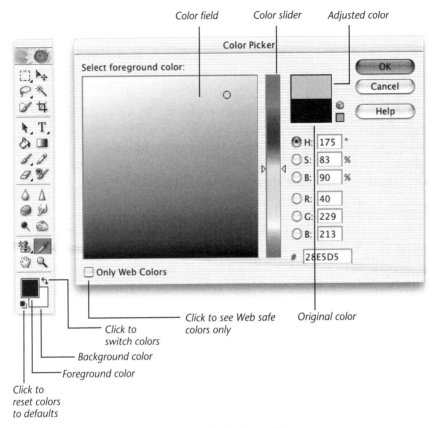

Color field   *Color slider*   *Adjusted color*

Color Picker

Select foreground color:

OK

Cancel

Help

H: 175 °
S: 83 %
B: 90 %

R: 40
G: 229
B: 213

28E5D5

Only Web Colors

Click to see Web safe colors only   *Original color*

Click to switch colors

Background color

Foreground color

Click to reset colors to defaults

Figure 6-2   *Specify a color of paint with the Color Picker.*

AS A MATTER OF FACT   The number values in the HSB or RGB fields of the Color Picker can be useful if you're trying to precisely match colors; otherwise, you can ignore them.

Once you see a range of desirable colors, click anywhere in the color field to choose a specific color. Watch the top color swatch as you pick different colors; it shows you a swatch of the new or adjusted color, while the swatch below it shows the original color. When you're pleased with your color choice, click OK.

Swatches Palette

If you only need one color of paint, you don't have to mess with a palette of colors. But most painters use lots of colors, and they have a tool (called an artist's palette) that's built to hold globs of these different paint colors. Then, each time they start a new work session, they can load up the palette with a new set of paint colors that are specific to that day's work. Elements has its own version of the artist's palette called the Swatches palette. To display it, go to **Window | Color Swatches**.

Choose a Color   While the Swatches palette has several libraries of color to choose from, you can view only one at a time—you probably see the Default library now (see Figure 6-3). If you like, you can change the view of your library from a list to a series of thumbnails. Just click the More button in the Swatches palette and select either Small Thumbnail or Small List (we prefer Small Thumbnails). Click a color in the palette to pick one; now it's the foreground color. And if you want to specify a new background color, **⌘**-click (Mac OS) or **CTRL**-click (Windows) a color in the palette.

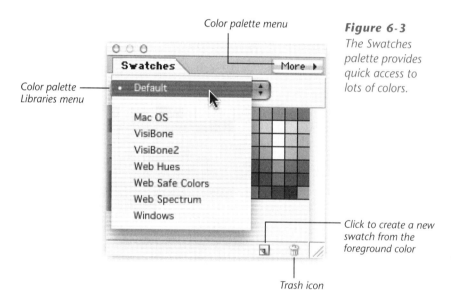

Color palette menu

Color palette Libraries menu

Figure 6-3
The Swatches palette provides quick access to lots of colors.

Click to create a new swatch from the foreground color

Trash icon

Choose a Library   Elements provides several preset color libraries. But, as we mentioned, you can only view one library at a time, so you'll occasionally want to switch from one library to another. To do that, click the Swatches palette pop-up menu and choose a library from the list. Try it now and select Web Safe Colors from the menu so you can see how the colors in the palette change. If you're working on an image you plan to post to the Web, this should be your library of choice.

While these preset color libraries are a good start, they're limited. It doesn't mean, however, that you're stuck with only those color palettes. In fact, the best part of the Swatches palette is that its libraries are customizable, so you can add and subtract colors and save libraries of your own. Say you've found a shade of blue in the Color Picker that you're especially fond of—you can simply add it to the Swatches palette for repeat usage.

Add Colors   Let's try it now. We'll add some colors to the library, so when we start painting, we won't have to return to the Color Picker each time we want to switch colors. Instead, we'll be able to select colors right from the Swatches palette. And since we know we're going to paint a landscape, we'll keep that in mind as we add colors to the palette.

1. Click the foreground color swatch in the Toolbox to open the Color Picker and choose a green that looks like lush grass.

2. In the Swatches palette, move the cursor to the gray area beneath the thumbnail color swatches (make sure the palette is in Thumbnail view mode); when it turns into the Paint Bucket icon, click OK.

3. Enter a name (if you like) in the Color Swatch Name dialog box and click OK. A new color swatch should appear in the Swatches Palette.

4. Repeat this process for as many colors as you think you'll need—maybe some more greens, a variety of blues, reds, yellows, and whatever else you like.

AS A MATTER OF FACT   *You can quickly sample colors from other images with the Eyedropper tool, just position its cursor over a color you like and click.*

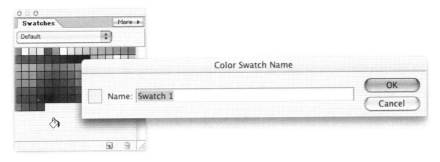

Figure 6-4   *Add and delete colors to customize a color library to your own needs.*

To save the colors you've added to a library, choose Save Swatches from the More menu in the Swatches palette. Enter a descriptive name, make sure the Color Swatches folder (it's in the Presets folder inside the Adobe Photoshop Elements folder) is designated as the destination, and click OK. The next time you restart the application, your new library should be in the Swatches palette library menu.

AS A MATTER OF FACT *To remove swatches from a library, drag the swatch to the Trash icon at the bottom of the Swatches palette. If you're sure you want the color removed from that library forever, resave the library.*

Choose a Brush

Now that you have a blank canvas and a palette of paints, we just need to talk about the paintbrushes. At the very least, you should know where to find them, how to tell one from another, and how to load them with paint. To that end, we'll just show you where to find the brushes and give you a few pointers. In the end, mastery of the brushes is up to you, so experiment and practice.

Select the Brush Tool

To start, click the Brush tool icon in the Toolbox, position the cursor over your canvas, then click and drag. You should notice that the Brush paints with the color that's specified as the foreground color (at the bottom of the Toolbox). The Brush worked as expected, but there's a lot more to consider than just color.

Any time you choose a tool from the Toolbox, you should make a pit stop at the Options bar before putting the tool to work. In the case of the Brush tool, it's where you can pick a brush size, a shape, and control how it behaves. The brush can be a big soft watercolor brush or a hard-edged, fine-tipped brush. It can even act like an airbrush or use different strengths of paint. We'll show you some important Options bar settings as we proceed, but for now, we just want to show how to find the various brushes at your disposal.

Brushes Pop-Up Palette

You have the Brush tool in hand, so now you need to decide how big or round or soft you want the tip to be. Click the brush sample in the Options bar (see Figure 6-5) to see the choices in the Brushes pop-up palette.

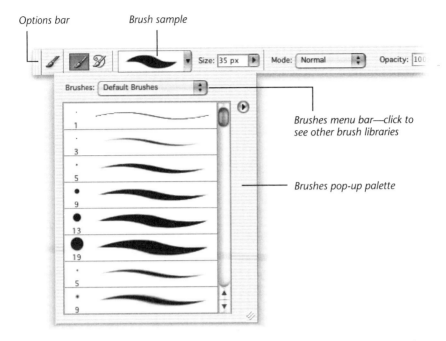

Options bar

Brush sample

Size: 35 px   Mode: Normal   Opacity: 100

Brushes: Default Brushes

Brushes menu bar—click to
see other brush libraries

Brushes pop-up palette

Figure 6-5 *Select a brush tip from the Brushes pop-up palette in the Options bar.*

But those aren't the only choices. To see the other available brush tip libraries, click the Brushes menu bar at the top of the palette (see Figure 6-5). Each library offers more brush choices—all told, there are dozens. In time, you'll find uses for some of the specialty brushes, like the Faux Finish or Special Effects Brushes; but for general use, the Default Brushes are a good choice—choose that set now. These brushes range from hard-edged to soft, large to small, and some even switch the brush to an airbrush or specialized shape. For now, choose a brush from the top portion of the Default Brush library, for all-purpose use.

AS A MATTER OF FACT *If you want to display the Brushes pop-up palette differently, click the triangle in the upper-right corner of the pop-up palette and select an alternate view option.*

Now, click a new color in the Swatches palette and drag this brush across the canvas. That's about all you need to know for basic painting technique: select a brush from the Brushes pop-up palette in the Options bar and choose paint colors. In the following section, we'll show you how to fine-tune the brushes while painting.

Erase

But first, we should clean the practice strokes off our canvas. Of course, at this point you could just click the Step Backward button to return to the blank canvas, but we'll take this opportunity to show you the Eraser tool. Select it from the Toolbox now—make sure you select the plain old Eraser, and not the Magic Eraser or the Background Eraser (they all share the same spot in the Toolbox).

> **AS A MATTER OF FACT** *The Magic Eraser and Background Eraser tools help remove large areas of color, but they're particularly helpful when working with photographs. If you'd like to learn more, consult Elements' Help feature.*

The Eraser tool is a little tricky. If you're working on the Background layer of a file as we are, erased pixels actually change to the background color. Since we want the pixels to change to white (the color of our canvas), we need to make sure the background color is set to white. The easiest way to do this is to click the icon at the bottom of the Toolbox that resets the foreground and background colors to their defaults (see Figure 6-2). Then click and drag the Eraser on the canvas until all your practice brush strokes are gone. You can change the size, shape, and opacity of the Eraser, just as you would a Brush, through the settings in the Options bar.

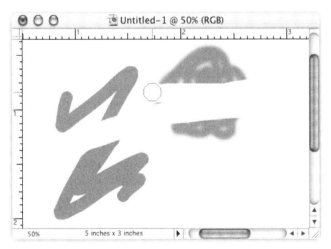

Figure 6-6
The Eraser tool behaves a lot like the Brush tool.

Paint to Canvas

It's time to start painting. The obvious choices to start with, of course, are the Brush tool or the Pencil. But those tools aren't efficient if you want to begin, as artists often do, by covering your canvas with color. Elements offers much better ways to fill large areas of color.

Fill With Paint

Even cheesy public television painters know that the most effective way to start a painting is to lay down large areas of color that suggest shapes and areas of interest. They know it's much easier to put paint on top of paint than to try to paint around things. For instance, for our landscape, we want to make the top portion of the painting blue (for sky) and the bottom portion green (for grass). We can go back and fill in the details and shading later. To start, we'll use two methods to fill large areas with color: the Gradient and Paint Bucket tools from the Toolbox.

Gradients

One of the easiest—and most interesting—ways to fill large areas with color is the Gradient tool; it creates a gradual blend of different colors. To try it, select the Gradient tool (to the right of the Paint Bucket) from the Toolbox and click the arrow next to the gradient sample in the Options bar (see Figure 6-7). Click the arrow in the upper right of the pop-up palette that appears, then choose Pastels from that menu.

Notice how the gradient choices in the pop-up palette change when you choose the Pastels gradient library; click one of these to select a specific gradient (we chose the Yellow, Green, Blue gradient). When you paint with any gradient, you should take note of the sequence of colors (yellow, then green, then blue) as they appear in the thumbnail; the gradient tool will always paint the colors in this order. So you can decide where these colors appear on your image by the way you drag the gradient tool across the canvas. For instance, if you start at the top of the image and drag down, your fill will start with yellow at the top and end with blue at the bottom. Since we want the top part of the sky to be blue, we'll drag in the opposite direction, from the bottom up. Position the cursor about one-half inch up from the bottom of the canvas, press **SHIFT** (this will prevent the gradient from skewing), click and drag to the top of the canvas, then release. Instant sky.

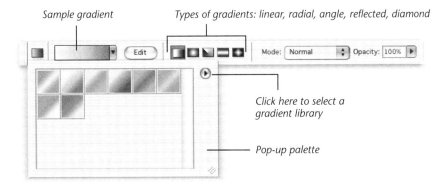

Sample gradient — Types of gradients: linear, radial, angle, reflected, diamond

Edit   Mode: Normal   Opacity: 100%

Click here to select a gradient library

Pop-up palette

Figure 6-7 *Gradients provide a fast and interesting solution for filling large areas with color.*

AS A MATTER OF FACT *Enabling the Dither option in the Options bar will help make your gradients as smooth as possible; however, banding can still occur (banding is when bands of color are visible in the gradient). To further combat banding after using a gradient: go to **Filter | Noise | Add Noise**, enter an amount between 1 to 4, select Gaussian, then click OK.*

Like many of Elements' features, it pays to experiment with Gradients because they can create all sorts of great effects. For instance, notice the row of icons next to the Gradient picker, which are the various types of gradients. We used a simple linear gradient to create our sky, but be sure to try the others. You should also know that any of the preset gradients are customizable. To change the color, shading, or gradation of a particular gradient, just click the Edit button to display the Gradient Editor, where you can adjust and then save any gradient to suit your needs.

Paint Bucket

Another simple way to fill large areas of color is by using the Paint Bucket tool. It's actually a rather crude and simple-minded tool, but it'll get the job done quickly if you just want to fill an area with a solid color. We'll use it to create a grassy meadow in the foreground of our landscape.

The paint bucket generally requires some parameters or borders; that is, it needs to know which areas of your image to fill. In our case, that means just an area across the bottom of our canvas. Let's start by creating a horizon line, and then we'll fill everything below it with color. To do the same:

1. Select a green from the Swatches palette, then click the Pencil tool icon in the Toolbox.

2. Enter a value of 5 in the Size field of the Options bar, and make sure the Auto Erase option is disabled (also in the Options bar).

3. Move the cursor to your canvas and draw (click and drag) a horizon line from left to right, about 1 inch up from the bottom—be sure to start and stop at the outermost edges of the canvas so there aren't any gaps in the line.

4. Select the Paint Bucket from the Toolbox, set the Tolerance (in the Options bar) to 100, and make sure the foreground color is green.

5. Move the cursor to a spot *below* the pencil line and click. The area should fill with color.

6. If the fill doesn't work as expected, use the Step Backward button to undo and check your pencil line for gaps; if you find gaps, touch them up with the pencil tool and try again.

Feel free to improvise here. Notice how, for our painting (see Figure 6-8), we drew an extra horizon line on the right side of our canvas to suggest hills. As long as there aren't any gaps in the pencil lines, the sections can be filled with different colors—we used two different shades of green to create the illusion of distance.

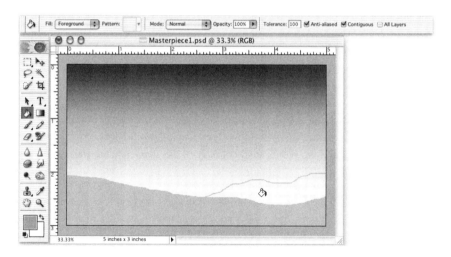

Figure 6-8 *Although a bit crude, the Paint Bucket tool can fill large areas with paint … fast.*

Customize a Brush

In general, the Paint Bucket tool has limited usefulness. But the same can't be said of the Brush tool; as you're about to see, it's remarkably flexible. Earlier in the chapter we gave you the quick version of painting with a brush: pick a foreground color, select the Brush from the Toolbox, and paint. We even showed you where to find the different brush tips, but there's a lot more to learn, so let's take a closer look.

Select the Brush tool from the Toolbox and look at the Options bar. Click the brush preview in the Options bar to open the Brushes pop-up palette (see Figure 6-9). As you saw earlier, all of the brushes are organized into categories. Now click the Brushes menu at the top of the pop-up palette and select Assorted Brushes. From those brushes, select Starburst Small to add stars to the sky.

Size

Before painting, choose a foreground and background color (at the bottom of the Toolbox) that will show up on the sky—we chose a very light blue and white. In the Options bar, enter a value of 100 in the Size field. We'll come back to the Size option shortly, to change the size of this brush again, but first, we want you to see this brush in action.

Go ahead and drag the brush across your canvas—little stars should appear, which is great, but a neat row of stars packed closely together is not the effect we're after, so we need to customize the brush a bit. Click the Step Backward button in the Shortcuts bar to undo the stars.

Spacing

To control the dynamics of any brush, click the More Options icon in the Options bar (see Figure 6-9). In this case, we're interested in the space between our stars, so we'll change the Spacing setting to about 400—watch the brush preview in the Options bar change dynamically as you change any brush settings.

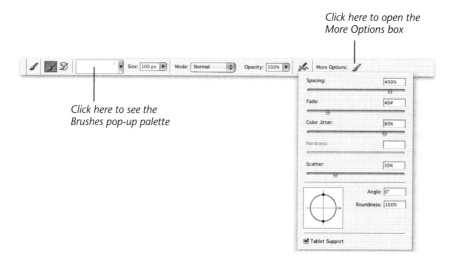

Click here to open the More Options box

Click here to see the Brushes pop-up palette

Figure 6-9   *The More Options settings give you control over the dynamics of a brush.*

If you like, you can investigate the other settings in the More Options pop-up menu. For instance, we altered our Starburst brush further by setting the Fade to 40, the Color Jitter to 80 percent, and the Scatter setting to 30 percent. For a primer on what each setting does to a brush, see the following list:

Spacing   A value greater than about 25 (the default) here will make the brush skip; the greater the value, the larger the gap between marks in the stroke.

Fade   The number here controls how many steps it takes to shut off the flow of paint completely; the brush stroke will gradually fade out to nothing—the greater the number, the slower the fade.

Color Jitter   Any number other than 0 will cause the brush to switch between the specified foreground and background color; the greater the number, the more frequent the switches.

Hardness   This setting controls the edges of the brush stroke; low numbers soften the edges of the brush and high numbers produce harder edges.

Scatter   The number here controls how marks in the brush stroke are scattered; the higher the setting, the more scattering occurs.

Angle and Roundness   You can either enter values in the fields or manipulate the diagram on the left to affect changes in the roundness of the brush or the angle of the stroke.

Now drag the brush across the canvas a couple of times to see the More Options settings changed the behavior of the brush. You can see how flexible the Brush tool becomes when coupled with the dozens of brush tips and controlled with the settings in the Options bar. And to drive home that point, we made a few more passes with the starburst brush:

1. Go back to the Options bar and change the Size of the brush to 200.

2. Swipe the brush across the sky a couple of times to add big stars here and there.

3. Then change the brush size to 70 and brush to add small stars as well.

AS A MATTER OF FACT *If you want to control the placement of each star, go back to the More Options box and set the Spacing to 0. Click here and there to add each star one at a time.*

Figure 6-10 *A starry night with just a few swipes of the Brush tool.*

Blend Colors

We could probably pass off our canvas as a painting, but it could be better. Sure, you can tell what it's supposed to be: grass and sky and stars. But you might want to mix and blend paint to create shading that adds depth and interest. If you want to go the extra mile, you have a couple of options: You can combine the Opacity and Fade settings of your brush, or you can use the Smudge tool to blend paint.

Opacity and Fade

When working with real paint on a canvas, you can control color by loading more or less paint onto your brush, especially in the case of watercolors. In Elements, you can approximate this effect by adjusting the Opacity setting in the Options bar. The default Opacity setting is 100 percent, which means your paint will be opaque or thick. Anything less than 100 percent will produce a more translucent effect, so some of the paint beneath the stroke will remain visible.

And the Fade setting—which we already used in the previous section—is a great way to blend new brush strokes into the colors underneath. You already know how this works—the Fade number controls how many steps it takes for the paint to fade as you drag the brush.

If you combine the two settings, you can produce a convincing simulation of real brushstrokes on a canvas. And if you add to that a specialized brush tip that imitates a real paintbrush, then the effect is furthered. To see what we mean:

1. Click the brush preview in the Options bar, and choose the Natural 2 library of brushes from the Brushes menu at the top of the palette.

2. Pick a brush—we chose the Wet Brush at the very bottom—from the library and set the Size to 40 and the Opacity to 50 percent.

3. Click the More Options icon in the Options bar and set the Fade to 25.

4. Select a color of paint from the Swatches palette (or the Color Picker), then click and drag the brush on your canvas to add shading here and there. Stop now and again to change the color of paint if you like.

Smudge

Another way to blend paints is with the Smudge tool; it's sort of like dragging a finger through wet paint because it grabs color from where you start (click) and then pushes it in the direction you drag. But if you enable the Finger Painting option in the Options bar, you can smudge a specified foreground color onto the image instead.

Select the Smudge tool now from the Toolbox (the pointing finger). If you like, you can select a brush tip and adjust the size, just as you did with the Brush tool. We selected the Faux Finish library of brushes, picked Texture Comb 1, and set the size to 70.

Figure 6-11 *Our finished painting, after some shading and the Smudge tool*

To control the strength of the smudge, try a Strength setting other than 100 percent in the Options bar—the lower the number, the more subtle the smudge. For instance, we started with a strength of 50 percent and changed it frequently. To blend existing colors in your painting, click and drag from one color to another—we started at the top of the green and moved the tool up, toward the sky. And to add more depth, we occasionally went back over the previous smudges or altered the Strength setting to get a variety of smudges. As you can see in Figure 6-11, the result looks like soft tufts of grass.

Mix Media

We've shown you how to create a painting from scratch, but it's important to remember that Elements is a great place to combine all sorts of stuff. We'll talk about this more in the next chapter, but for now, it's enough to emphasize that you can combine the paint techniques you just learned with photos—we'll show you a couple of useful examples now.

Colorize an Image

Another way to mix it up in Elements is to use the Brush tool to colorize a photograph. You can use this technique to add color to a black-and-white photo, or change and enhance existing colors in a photograph.

Open a photo and select the Brush tool. The Options bar settings are up to you, with one exception: Choose Color from the Mode menu in the Options bar. Now the brush will use the color of paint (the foreground color) to replace what's in the photo without losing any detail. Try it to see what we mean. This is a great way to add new life to faded old photos. Try the other Mode settings, like Multiply or Overlay, to achieve different effects as you paint over photos with the Brush tool.

> **AS A MATTER OF FACT** *If you're coloring an old black-and-white photo, go to* **Image | Mode | RGB** *to be sure you're not using Grayscale mode. Otherwise, you won't see any color no matter how much you paint.*

Turn a Photo Into a Painting

Another way to combine photos and paint tools is to use the Impressionist Brush, which shares the same space in the Toolbox as the Brush tool. While it's a brush of sorts, it works differently than the Brush tool in one important way: It manipulates existing pixels, rather than adding pixels. Since this is the case, you need some pixels to start with—either something you previously painted or an image file, like a digital photo.

Impressionist Brush

The Impressionist Brush tool rearranges the pixels in an image to simulate impressionistic brush strokes, rather than using the foreground or background colors to paint new pixels. To try it, first open an existing image or use the canvas you painted in the earlier parts of this chapter.

Click and hold the Brush tool icon in the Toolbox to reveal the hidden Impressionist Brush tool (the paintbrush with a swirl), and select it. Click the brush sample in the Options bar and choose the Default category of brushes from the pop-up palette's menu. Then choose a simple round brush tip from the Default category.

Figure 6-12   *Before ... and after using the Impressionist Brush.*

Adjust the size of the brush in the Options bar (Size field), but leave the Mode set to Normal and the Opacity set to 100 percent for now. To control the Impressionist Brush's effects, click the More Options button and specify the following options:

- The Style setting controls the shape of the stroke.
- The value in the Area field refers to the area that will be covered by the strokes; the greater the number here, the larger the area covered.
- The Tolerance setting controls where strokes are applied to an image. For instance, the brush affects pixels within a range of color values (the Tolerance setting), relative to the color of the pixel you click. If the Tolerance is set to a low number, and you click a yellow part of the image, only the pixels of a very similar color (yellow) will be affected. A larger Tolerance setting will produce the effect on pixels that have a wider range of colors.

Now you can drag the brush over your image to see what happens. If you don't like the effect, use the Step Backward button in the Shortcuts bar to undo it, then revisit the settings in the Options bar to try again.

The paint tools you've used in this chapter do some of their best work when enhancing, manipulating, or otherwise doing weird and interesting things to existing images. In fact, much of the excitement in using Elements comes when you begin to combine images and mix media. In the next chapter we'll show you how to combine images in all sorts of interesting ways; you'll use many of the skills you've learned so far and pick up several new ones to add to your bag of tricks.

Combine Images

One of the most flexible aspects of editing images in Photoshop Elements is the ability to combine images through the use of *layers*. Of course, if you're using Elements for simple tasks—cropping and resizing images, removing a few specks of dust, or printing to your color printer—you can manage without adding layers to images. But if you want to do more sophisticated edits—add color to images, apply special effects, or add your nephew's head to a dog's body—a basic understanding of layers is vital. In fact, layers offer tremendous flexibility when used in conjunction with Elements' image editing tools and commands. This flexibility, coupled with the complex effects they facilitate, will let you combine images in ways you never imagined.

You got a sneak peek at layers in previous chapters, but there's more to understand. Imagine a composite image made up of three pieces of clear plastic, uniform in size, stacked one on top of the other. Imagine that each piece of plastic (layer) contains one part of that composition. For example, the bottom layer is a background covered from edge to edge with beautiful blue sky and a grassy pasture. The middle layer depicts a lonesome cow. And the third (top) layer contains text. When combined, the composite image is of a talking cow enjoying a beautiful day in a grassy meadow. That's a basic understanding of layers and how they work.

You'll learn in this chapter how easy it is to make changes with layers. For instance, if you're fickle and decide a chicken should replace the cow in that field of greens, layers make changing it painless. Simply replace the cow layer with a new one that contains a chicken. Replace the blue sky with a tornado. Replace the grassy knoll with a lunar landscape. You can add, delete, distort, and blend layers into one another. And what's more, each layer remains independent so you can change one without affecting others.

Build a Layered File

To illustrate some of the principles covered in this chapter, we'll combine images to create something useful. Let's say we need a poster to announce a neighborhood barbecue. A poster usually contains many different visual elements, so it's a perfect opportunity to illustrate the flexibility and power of layers. And the techniques we'll demonstrate can be used to combine all sorts of images—you could make a collage of those old family photos, create campaign buttons for your daughter's bid for student council president, or paste your husband into a photo with Winston Churchill and F.D.R. And since all layered compositions need a background, that's where we'll start.

Create a Background

Photoshop Elements provides several options to create a background for a layered image—you can draw, paint, or import images from scanners and digital cameras—but the easiest option is to open an existing image. Do that now. We chose an image of a field and blue sky, but you can choose anything you'd like.

> **AS A MATTER OF FACT** *Stock photographs can be found in a folder called Stock Art on the Elements install CD-ROM.*

With an image open, find the Layers tab in the Palette Well (if you can't find it, go to **Window | Layers**). Click the tab, hold the mouse button, and then drag the palette down to your Work Area. Moving the Layers palette to the Work Area like this will give you a handy and ever-present view of your layered file. If you look at the palette now, you'll see one layer that's named *Background*—this is how Elements starts every file. The Background layer remains the bottom layer of an image and, for the most part, cannot be altered—the lock icon that appears in the palette indicates that the layer is locked to most changes.

> **AS A MATTER OF FACT** *If you think you'll want to move or edit the Background layer down the road, double-click its name in the Layers palette and name it something else. That converts it to an editable layer.*

Figure 7-1
Start a layered
file with a
background.

Layers palette

Background layer

Add a Shape

A layer can contain all manner of things: text, photographic images, scanned objects, or images you create using Elements' paint and draw tools. In our example we'll use a combination of tools from the Toolbox, starting with a Shape tool.

To draw a simple shape, click the Shape tool icon in the Toolbox (see Figure 7-2), and hold down the mouse button until you see the menu of hidden Shape tools, then choose the Rectangle shape tool. To draw the shape, click and drag the cursor from one side of your file to the other—draw a rectangle an inch or two high, across the width of the file.

> **AS A MATTER OF FACT** Don't forget to try the other Shape tools. The Custom Shape tool, for instance, lets you create great shapes from the many Custom Shape libraries that are available from the Options bar.

When you use a Shape tool, you use vector technology. And if you remember our discussion of vector art (Chapter 2), you'll remember that vector art's biggest advantage is that it can be resized without a loss in detail or in crispness of edges. What's more, you'll notice that the Shape tools automatically create a new layer for you, which makes a change to the color and size easy. To show you how easy it is, we'll change the color of our rectangle.

Change Color

Look for the layer named "Shape 1" in the Layers palette—that's the layer that contains the shape you just drew. Look to the left of that layer's name in the Layers palette—that little box is called the layer *thumbnail* and it's just that, a thumbnail of what that layer contains. To change the color of the shape:

1. Double-click the shape layer's thumbnail in the Layers palette.

2. Pick a light yellow color from the Color Picker box (see Chapter 6 for help).

3. Click OK.

> **AS A MATTER OF FACT**   *If you want to change the color of the shape to a gradient fill or a pattern fill, go to **Layer | Change Layer Content | Gradient** (or **Pattern**) and choose the options you want from the dialog box that pops up.*

Simplify Layer

We like this rectangle as it is—we're sure we won't need to change its size and color later, so we can convert it to a bitmap layer. As with any shape created by a Shape tool (as well as type), you can and should convert the art from vector to bitmap art before you're finished with a file. This is important, because as long as the art is vector, you won't be able to use certain filters, effects, or paint tools on it. Let's convert the rectangle now so you can see how.

Click the layer's name in the Layers palette to make sure it's active (you should see the Paintbrush icon), then go to **Layer | Simplify Layer**. That's it. The important thing to remember—whether *simplifying* a shape or type layer—is that you shouldn't do this until you're sure you won't need to change the type formatting or the shape's size and color. Once you simplify a layer, those changes become either difficult or impossible to make.

Add Type

We could continue to add layer upon layer, but for now let's just add one more that contains type (see Chapter 5 for a full discussion of type). Select the Type tool from the Toolbox, click the Image Area, type anything you want, and then press **ENTER**—we typed the date and time of our barbecue. When you use the Type tool, Elements automatically creates a new layer and names it for you (the type layer's name reflects the content of the text in the layer), as with the Shape tools.

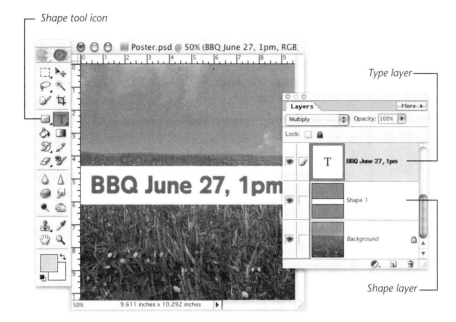

Shape tool icon

Type layer

Shape layer

Figure 7-2 *Our barbecue poster begins to take shape with the addition of a type layer.*

You should now have three layers: a Background layer, a Shape layer, and a type layer on top. Those are the basics of creating a layered file. Sure, it's a simple layered file, but it's a good start and it will go a long way toward illustrating the principles covered in the following sections.

Understand Layers

Having come this far, it's likely you already have a firm grasp of how layers are like sheets of clear plastic stacked in a neat pile. You've also seen how you put parts of your composition on different layers, and we've introduced you to the Layers palette. But because the Layers palette is such an important feature, let's pause and take a closer look at it right now, before we move on to more complex topics.

Layers Palette

As layers in a file multiply, so does the potential for losing track of what's what in a composition. Fortunately, the Layers palette provides a handy visual inventory of a layered file. It lists the layers in your file from top to bottom—the top layer in the palette is the top layer in your stack of images.

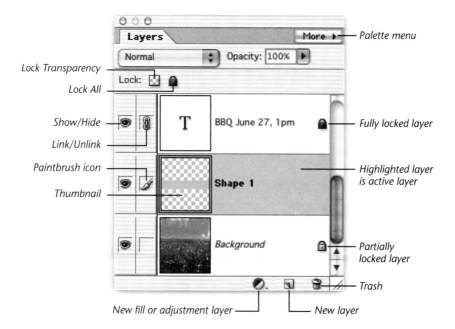

Figure 7-3   *The Layers palette keeps a visual inventory of a layered file.*

In the main body of the palette, you should see four columns: one with the Eye icon, one with the Paintbrush icon, one with a thumbnail view of the layer's contents, and one with the name of the layer. There's lots of other information in the palette, but for now, let's concentrate on the icons since they provide important cues and clues for us to follow.

The first icon you probably noticed is the Eye icon, which indicates a layer's visibility. Simply click it to show or hide a layer's contents in the Image Window. Turn the visibility of the Shape layer off and on to try it now.

AS A MATTER OF FACT   *If you print from a layered file, only visible layers will print.*

Next to the Eye icon, you should see a Paintbrush icon in the Layers palette, which indicates a layer that is *active* and ready to be manipulated. And since only one layer can be active at a time, you'll only see one Paintbrush icon at a time in the palette. But to get around this limitation, you can link layers to one another so they can be transformed and moved as a group. When you link layers, the column that displays the Paintbrush icon will also display the Link icon. We'll show you how to link layers later in this chapter.

The next column to the right displays a Thumbnail image of each layer's contents. You can customize this thumbnail view by selecting Palette Options from the palette menu (see Figure 7-4).

AS A MATTER OF FACT *If you'd like a more spartan Layers palette, reduce the size of the thumbnails or eliminate them completely. This not only saves space in the palette, but also reduces the memory requirements of your file.*

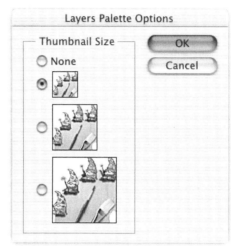

Figure 7-4
Customize the thumbnails in the Layers palette.

The last column in the Layers palette contains a layer's name, which can be changed at any time by double-clicking the name in the palette. It's good practice to use descriptive names such as "blue sky with clouds" or "lone brown cow" for layers as you create them, to prevent confusion down the road.

In the bottom-right corner of the Layers palette you should see three icons: New Fill or Adjustment layer, New layer, and Trash. To add a fill or adjustment layer to your file, click the New Fill or Adjustment Layer icon. (See Chapter 3 for more on fill and adjustment layers.) To add a new blank layer, click the New Layer icon. To delete a layer, select the target layer and click the Trash icon. There are also some additional features at the top of the Layers palette: drop-down menus and the lock functions. Take note of these for now—we'll demonstrate their uses later in the chapter.

Arrange Objects

Now that you know your way around the Layers palette, let's put it to good use. We'll start by arranging the elements of the composition, since it's an important and practical use of a layered file's flexibility. For instance, you can reposition objects in the Image Window, place them in front or behind one another, and even link them so they'll move as a unit.

Move

Let's move the type layer a bit to demonstrate how to reposition the contents of layers. Click the type layer's name in the Layers palette to activate it (notice the Paintbrush icon in the Layers palette) and select the Move tool from the Toolbox. Position the cursor over the type, then click and drag the layer around the Image Window. Any layer that's not locked can be moved in this manner, so it's a quick and easy way to experiment with a composition. Position your type so it partially overlaps the rectangle and is centered horizontally.

Figure 7-5 *Drag a layer with the Move tool to reposition it.*

AS A MATTER OF FACT *Try to do just about anything to the Background layer and Elements will tell you that it "Could not complete this...." This is because Background layers are always partially locked to alterations.*

Reorder

Not only can you easily reposition the contents of a layer in the composition, you can also reposition each layer in the *stacking order*. The stacking order corresponds to the list of layers, from top to bottom, in the Layers palette. Look at the Layers palette now to see what we mean, then grab the Type layer's name and drag it to a new position in the Layers palette (just below the Shape layer). You just changed the stacking order of your layers. The type layer should now be partially obscured by the rectangle, which is on the layer above.

> **AS A MATTER OF FACT**   *A Background layer cannot be repositioned in the stacking order of a layered file.*

To better understand the concept of stacking order, take a look at the thumbnail of the layer named Shape 1 in the Layers palette. The checkerboard pattern you see in the thumbnail indicates transparent areas of a bitmap layer (vector layers do not show this in the thumbnail until they are simplified). In this case, those transparent areas explain why parts of the type layer are visible, even though its position in the stacking order is now below the shape layer, as seen in Figure 7-6.

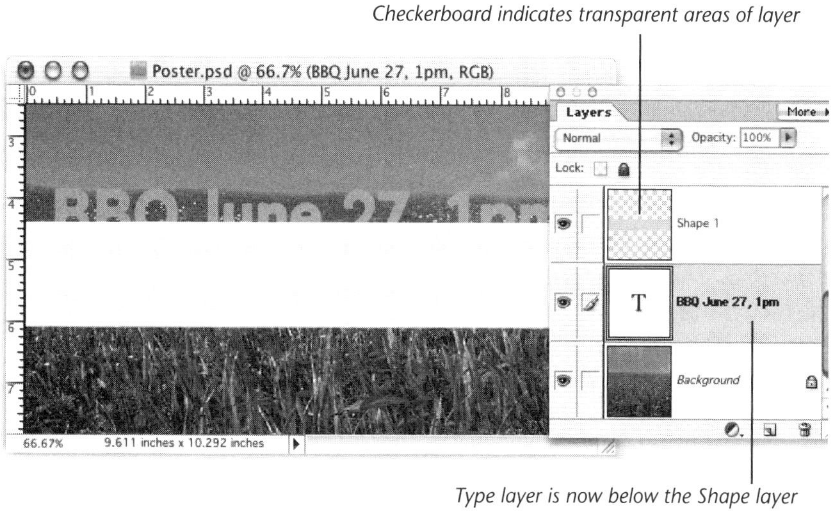

Checkerboard indicates transparent areas of layer

Type layer is now below the Shape layer

Figure 7-6   *The Type layer, after it's repositioned in the stacking order, is now partially obscured by the layer above it.*

Link

For our poster, we want both the rectangle and the type to appear near the bottom of the image. Although we could reposition the layers individually, it'll be much easier if we *link* them, so they can be moved as a unit.

But first, return the Type layer to its original position in the stacking order and center the type in the rectangle. To link the two layers, activate the Type layer, then click the paintbrush/link column of the Shape layer. Now the two layers can be moved in unison with the Move tool. And if you want to unlink the layers, just click the link icon in the Layers palette to make it disappear.

Blend Images

You now know the basics of adding and arranging layers, so you're ready to tackle a more complex concept, like *blending modes.* A blending mode lets you control how one layer's pixels blend with the pixels of underying layers. And since there are many different blending modes, you have to use the Blending Modes pop-up menu to tell Elements which one you'd like to use.

You'll find the Blending Modes pop-up menu in the upper-left side of the Layers palette (see Figure 7-7). Of the many choices available, you may find that only a handful suit your needs. To illustrate, select the Shape layer to make it active and then select Screen from the Blending Modes pop-up menu, as seen in Figure 7-7. In essence, this choice tells the active layer how to blend its pixels with the pixels of the layer underneath.

As a general rule, the effects of blending modes are difficult to predict, so our advice is to experiment—you'll soon get a feel for which ones you like and dislike. We're fond of Multiply, Screen, Overlay, Soft Light, and Color Burn. But you might prefer Dissolve, Darken, and Hue.

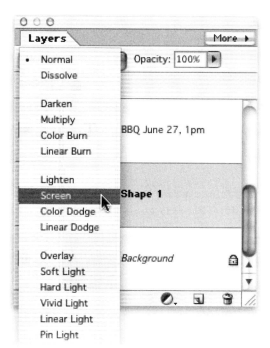

Figure 7-7
The Blending Modes pop-up menu is found in the Layers palette.

AS A MATTER OF FACT *Only one blending mode can be applied at a time, but they can be changed from one to another at any time.*

Make an Image Transparent

Another way to control the way layers interact with each other is to make a layer partially transparent, so the layer beneath becomes partially visible. To demonstrate, with your Shape layer still active, enter 85 percent in the Opacity field (upper-right side of the Layers palette). The lower the value entered in this box, the more transparent the contents of that layer will be. The default for any layer is 100 percent, but it can be changed any time and it can be different from layer to layer.

Now we've set up a complex interaction between layers. We've combined the blending mode applied in the last section with an alteration to the opacity of that same layer, to achieve a more dramatic and interesting effect. And in our example, we added another layer into the mix by assigning the Multiply blending mode to the Type layer. Imagine all the possibilities: Knowing that just about any layer can be combined with any other, you can create really great effects in just a few simple steps.

Figure 7-8
Set up complex interactions among layers to achieve more compelling results.

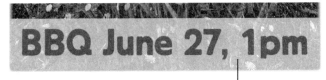

Background layer is now partially visible ⎤

AS A MATTER OF FACT   *Remember, the Background layer of a file will not accept most modifications. The Opacity setting is one case in point—you cannot change the opacity of the Background layer of a file.*

Mask an Image

A *mask* lets you hide or protect specific areas of a layer's contents—it's like defining a sort of force field. There are two easy ways to mask an image in Photoshop Elements. You can tell Elements to hide parts of an image, or you can tell Elements to leave the transparent parts of a layer unchanged. We'll show you how to do both.

Lock Transparency

Remember the checkerboard pattern we discussed in the Reorder section of this chapter? The checkerboard indicates the transparent areas of a layer (areas without pixels) and when you select a layer and click the Lock Transparency check box (in the upper-left corner of the Layers palette), that layer's transparent areas become locked to changes. As long as a layer is partially locked in this manner, the transparent areas are protected as if covered by a stencil or a mask.

To demonstrate, let's create a new layer that contains type. We added "BYOB" to the top of our poster and then selected **Layer | Simplify Layer** to convert the type to artwork (because you cannot lock the transparency of a Type layer). With this new layer active, click the Lock Transparency check box in the Layers palette (see Figure 7-2). The transparent areas around the letters "BYOB" are now locked to changes. Select the Paintbrush tool and paint on your new type layer to see what we mean. You should find that changes occur only to the areas that already contain pixels (the letters), as shown in Figure 7-9.

Round paintbrush used ───

Figure 7-9
Lock transparency to protect transparent parts of a layer.

Group Layers

Just as the transparent areas of a layer can act as a sort of stencil or mask when its partially locked, a similar effect can be achieved by *grouping* layers together. And the perfect use for this kind of mask is to crop a photograph to the shape of a letter, a word, or any shape at all. To show you what we mean, we'll group our "BYOB" type layer with an image that looks like drops of liquid on glass. But first we need to open and then copy and paste the new image into our poster file. So with both files open and the new image file active, go to **Select | All** and then **Edit | Copy**. Activate the destination file (the poster in our case) and select **Edit | Paste**. Elements automatically adds a layer to receive the new image we pasted.

To understand grouping, you should know that when you group two or more layers, the bottom or *base layer* becomes the boundary or outline for other layers in the group. This base layer or boundary is the shape of the mask. You can make just about anything your base layer, even type, as long as the base layer contains some transparent areas.

Since we want the image we just pasted (the drops of liquid) to appear only in the shape of the letters "BYOB", we'll make "BYOB" our base layer by making sure its position in the stacking order is just below the drops of liquid layer. Then we'll link the two layers and select **Layers | Group Layers**. That's it. Now the base layer, "BYOB" in our case, acts as a mask for the Drops layer, as shown in Figure 7-10.

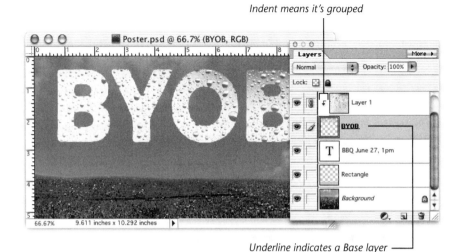

Indent means it's grouped

Underline indicates a Base layer

Figure 7-10 *Layers that are grouped take on the shape of the Base (bottom) Layer.*

To remove a layer from the group at any time, select the layer and then **Layer |
Ungroup**. This removes the selected layer and any layers above it from the group.
To ungroup all layers, select the base layer and then **Layer | Ungroup**.

Add Image Layers

In the previous section you learned how to copy an image from another file and
then paste it into a new layer in a working file, as we did with the drops of liquid in
the Group Layers section. But there are a couple of other ways to add new image
layers to a file.

Duplicate Layers

If you just want to duplicate a layer within your file, simply grab the layer's name in
the Layers palette and drag it to the New Layer icon at the bottom of the palette
(see Figure 7-2). Notice that the name of the new layer is the same, with "copy"
added to the end. You can change this name by double-clicking on the layer's name.

Drag Layers

But if you want your new image layer to contain the contents of a layer from
another image file, you can drag it from one file to another, bypassing the copy
and paste commands. With both files open, click a layer's name in the source file's
Layers palette, then drag it to the destination file's Image Window, as shown in

Figure 7-11. When you see a dark border appear around the destination file's Image Window, release the mouse button to drop the copy into the file. We think this is the easiest way to copy a layer from one file to another, so we used it to add a cow to our poster.

Figure 7-11 *Grab, drag, and drop to copy an image from one file into another.*

We should mention that the cow in our image was already isolated from its original background. If you want to learn how to isolate objects for your composition, see Chapter 4 for a discussion of selection techniques.

Clean It Up

Now that we've positioned the cow in the composition, we're pleased with the results and ready to print our posters and hang them in the neighborhood. But first, we should clean up our file a bit. After all, as you add layer upon layer and image upon image, a file's bound to become a little unwieldy, which can result in huge file sizes. So it's important to remember that each time you add a layer you increase a file's size. And the larger the file's size, the slower it will open, accept edits, and save. You should also remember that the more layers you add to a file, the greater the potential for confusion and frustration. In this section we'll provide tips and examples of good layer management to help you prevent these potential problems.

Lock

Occasionally you may find that you're satisfied with a particular layer as it is, but want to continue working on other layers in the file. To protect a layer from all changes, click a layer's name in the Layers palette and click the Lock All check box in the upper-left corner of the palette. A solid black lock icon to the right of the layer's name indicates that a layer is fully locked and no image editing can take place, although it can still be repositioned in the stacking order.

Delete

If you know you no longer need a layer, dump it. It will reduce the file size, allow images to open and save faster, and filters or complex tasks will perform more efficiently. To delete a layer, select it in the Layers palette and click the Trash icon at the bottom of the palette. Click OK when Elements displays a dialog box that politely asks for confirmation, as shown in Figure 7-12.

Figure 7-12
Elements asks you to confirm the deletion of a layer.

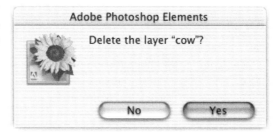

AS A MATTER OF FACT *It's easy to lose sight of what's really important—file size. Try to manipulate a file that's 250MB and you might run up against some memory limitations. Some files are simply too big. Remember that each time you add a layer to a file, you increase the file size, which eventually decreases performance.*

Merge

Another way to reduce file size and complexity is to combine or *merge* layers. When you're ready to commit to parts of an image as they appear in your file, you can tell Elements to compress the targeted layers into one layer. To do this, link the layers you want to merge and select Merge Linked from the Layers palette menu.

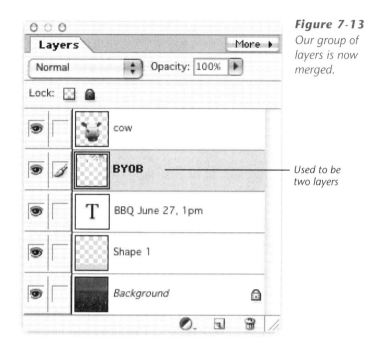

Figure 7-13
Our group of layers is now merged.

Used to be two layers

Flatten

If you really want to commit, you can flatten all layers at once. While it has its benefits (it cuts file sizes dramatically), flattening a file makes even the most experienced Elements user hesitate—once you save a flattened file you can no longer edit layers and move elements with ease. For this reason, we recommend you flatten files only at the very end of the image-editing process, when you're sure you're ready to commit.

To flatten a file, select Flatten Image from the Layers palette menu. No matter how many layers you started with, you end up with one. That's it. However, there is a way to make sure you're never caught wishing you hadn't flattened a file. You can keep a layered version as well as a flattened version. This is a good habit when working with complex files.

Flattened to one layer

Figure 7-14 *Our finished and flattened file*

Save As

The best method (if you have enough storage space) is to save both a flattened file and a layered version. To do so, make sure all your layers are visible, then choose **File | Save As**. You can enter a name for your file or let Elements name it for you. Choose TIFF from the pop-up Format menu. In this case, the TIFF file format does not support layers so Elements flattens the file for you when you select Save. And, because you chose to Save As, you still have the original layered version of the file. (See Chapter 9 for more on the Save As command and file formats.)

Make a Panorama

You've made it through the hard stuff—learning how to combine images through the use of layers. But we want to show you one more way to combine images, and it doesn't involve layers at all. In fact, in this case Elements does all of the hard work for you. And because it's so easy to do, we wanted to save it for last; consider it a reward.

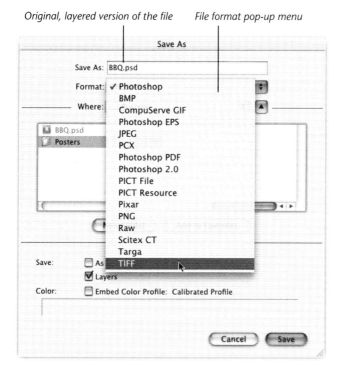

Figure 7-15
Use the Save As command to save a flattened copy of a layered file.

Using a built-in command, you can combine two or more images to make a panorama. The bad news is that unless you have a camera (either digital or traditional) with a tripod, this command may be of no interest to you. But if you do, Elements makes it remarkably easy. The hardest part is taking the pictures. But once you've done that, you can simply use the Photomerge command to stitch your images together into one file.

Here's how it works: Say you have a tripod, a camera, and a scene you want to shoot. With Elements and a little bit of planning, you can create a beautiful panorama in no time. But before you start snapping the individual shots that will be stitched together, keep the following guidelines in mind:

- Use a tripod with a swiveling head.
- Stay in the same spot as you take each photo.
- Use the same exposure for each shot.
- Don't use a distorting lens.
- Use a consistent focal length for each shot (don't use a zoom lens).
- Overlap each shot by about 25 percent.

In our example, we took three shots of a lake scene, all from the same vantage point, swiveling the camera on the tripod a little bit with each shot. And since we used a traditional camera, we scanned the photos and saved them to our computer's hard drive. Once you either load your digital files or scan the traditional prints, start Elements and go to **File | Create Photomerge**.

The next thing you'll see is the Photomerge dialog box (Figure 7-16). Click the Browse button in the box, find an image file, click Open, and then repeat until you've included all of the files you want to include in the panorama. When all your files show up in the Source Files window, click OK. This tells Elements which files it should stitch together into a panorama.

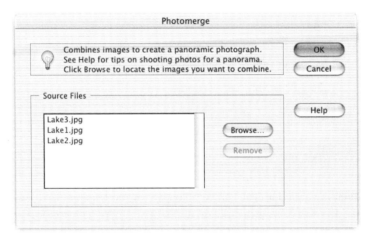

Figure 7-16   *Click the Browse button to tell Elements which files you'd like to stitch together.*

If the panorama cannot be automatically stitched together, Elements will politely notify you. But don't worry, all's not lost, because you can stitch images together manually from the next Photomerge box that appears (Figure 7-17). The first thing you'll notice is the preview you see of the panorama. But in our case, Elements could not include the last piece of the puzzle for some reason, so it stitched together only the first two files. The third file is stored for us in the Lightbox, just above the Work Area.

To move the image from the Lightbox to the Work Area, we selected the Image tool and then dragged the image from the Lightbox to the Work Area, approximating its final position in the composition—as long as the Snap to Image option is enabled, the image will snap into place and Elements will automatically blend the image into the composition.

You could even use this Lightbox to store parts of the panorama you want to remove from the composition—just select the Image tool (the pointer) and grab an image from the preview and drag it to the Lightbox. You can even fine-tune the placement of a section, rotate it, or fine-tune the perspective, all from this box. However, if you shoot your photos with care, the Photomerge command should work seamlessly, and you won't need to fiddle with any adjustments. Just click OK and save the resulting panorama as an Elements file.

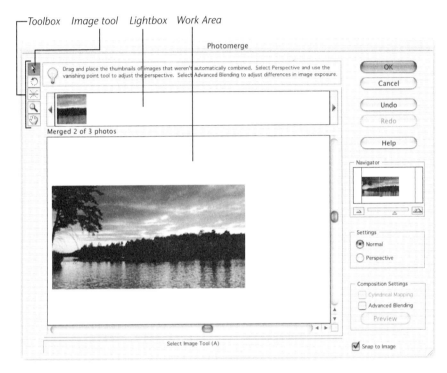

Figure 7-17 *The second Photomerge box lets you fine-tune a composition before committing to it.*

By now you know about retouching, combining, and painting images. And you're probably already convinced that Elements is the place to go when you need to do just about anything. But there is one more thing we should show you: How to put finishing touches on images, to take them that extra step. That's what we'll demonstrate in the next chapter.

Embellish

In Chapter 7 you learned how to combine images to create compositions. Add to those skills the tools that Elements provides for embellishing images, and you'll start to feel like a graphics pro. Want to make a photo of your best girl look like an impressionist painted it? Apply the Smudge Stick filter. Want to make something look like it's under water? Try one of the Distort filters. In this chapter, we'll show you how to get eye-popping results or subtle variations in an image with just a few mouse clicks.

Don't misunderstand: applying filters isn't the only way to enliven your images; they're just the beginning. We'll also show you how to use Elements' built-in effects and layer styles to enhance an image. And once you get acquainted with each of these features, you can combine them with one another to achieve dramatic results.

Keep in mind that experimentation is the house rule (ours, anyway). Like so many other things in Photoshop Elements, filters, effects, and layer styles can produce unpredictable results, especially when you combine them. But there's no pass or fail here—not even a test. Use our examples as guidance and repeat after us: "I can always undo what I've done by using the Step Backward button on the Shortcuts bar or the Undo History palette." (See Chapter 1 for more on this.)

Be an Artist

With Photoshop Elements you can be an artist without picking up a paintbrush or putting on a smock. No messy cleanup and no exorbitant rent for an airy studio in Paris. All you need is a picture to manipulate and a handful of filters.

Filters

The easiest way to make an image look like a master painting (or drawing) is to use a filter—especially the Artistic and Brush Stroke filters. These are just two of the many categories you'll see in the Filters palette in the Palette Well. Open an existing image and drag the Filters palette down from the Palette Well. In the top left of the palette, you should see a pop-up menu; click it to see the list of filter categories. The folks at Adobe, when faced with the dozens of filters they wanted to include, courteously organized them into loose groupings or categories.

To see what we mean, select Artistic to view the Artistic filters and then select Brushstrokes to view the Brushstrokes filters. Notice that when you select a category from the pop-up menu, the options in the palette change to display only the filters for that category. If you like, you can view all filters at once by choosing All from the menu, but you'll probably find it easier to view the filters by category.

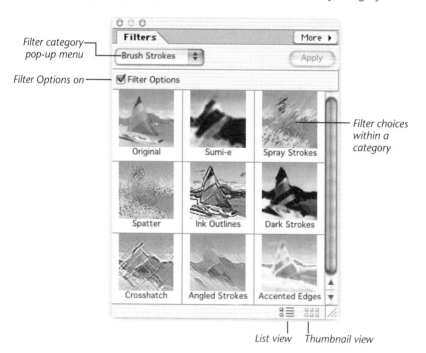

Filter category pop-up menu

Filter Options on

Filter choices within a category

List view   *Thumbnail view*

Figure 8-1   *The Filters palette*

Now click the List View icon in the bottom right of the Filters palette (see Figure 8-1). We like the List View option because it keeps things tidy, but if you prefer bigger thumbnail views, click the Thumbnail View icon. Either way, the palette shows a preview of the effect each filter will produce.

AS A MATTER OF FACT *If you're using lots of filters and effects, you might want to dock one palette to the other to save space on your screen. (See Chapter 1 to learn how to dock palettes.)*

Now that you understand how the filters are organized, let's put some to use. As we've said, the Artistic and Brushstrokes filter categories are designed specifically to make a picture look like a work of art—they use brush strokes and textures to achieve realistic effects. You can also get similar results with a variety of filters, even ones that don't appear in the two categories we've mentioned (like the Sketch category of filters). But if you want to be an artist right out of the gate, the Artistic and Brushstrokes filters are the obvious choices.

Impressionist

While we can't easily reproduce Manet's *Olympia* with filters, we can reproduce the loose and spontaneous brush strokes that came to characterize the movement known as Impressionism. In short, we can copy Manet's style. But to start, we need an image to play with. Any image will do, so we chose a simple image of clouds to illustrate.

AS A MATTER OF FACT *Many of the images used throughout this book can be found in a folder called Stock Art on the Elements install CD-ROM.*

Figure 8-2
Before ... and after the Angled Strokes filter

The point here is to suggest actual brush strokes and paint so we used the Angled Strokes option from the Brush Strokes category of filters. Here's how you can achieve similar effects:

1. Open an image and pull the Filters palette down from the Palette Well.

2. Choose Brush Strokes from the pop-up menu in the upper-left side of the palette (see Figure 8-1).

3. Select the Angled Strokes filter from the options shown in the palette.

4. Click the Filter Options box in the upper-left side of the Filters palette (see Figure 8-1) to turn off this option.

5. With the Angled Strokes filter selected, click Apply and watch your image change.

AS A MATTER OF FACT *Filters can be applied only to active and visible layers. And they can't be applied to Bitmap-mode or Indexed-color images; if your image is either one, change the mode to RGB or Grayscale. (See Chapter 2 for help with color modes.)*

If you don't like the results of the Angled Strokes filter, use the Step Backward button to undo the filter and try another. For example, you can also achieve an Impressionist look with the Palette Knife, Paint Daubs, or Smudge Stick filters from the Artistic category.

Surrealist

If Impressionists bore you, you might prefer the warped and twisted reality of a Surrealist like Salvador Dalí with the help of the Liquify filter. Open an image, select Distort from the pop-up menu of filter categories, and double-click the Liquify filter. It operates a little differently than other filters in that it has its own toolbox and image work area where you show the filter how to behave (see Figure 8-3).

The full-screen window that popped up shows a preview of your entire image, a toolbox on the left, and some controls on the right-hand side of the work area. Select the Warp tool (the paintbrush at the top of the Toolbox) and set the Brush Size to 100 and the Brush Pressure to 100 in the Tool Options section (upper-right side) of the window. Drag the tool across your image preview to watch it change. Now click Revert and set the Brush Pressure to 20. This time when you drag the tool you should notice a difference. No matter which tool you use, the lower the Brush Pressure setting, the slower the changes occur. So to start, keep this setting somewhere around 50 to better control your transformations. Click Revert again to undo the last change, then try each of the tools in the toolbox.

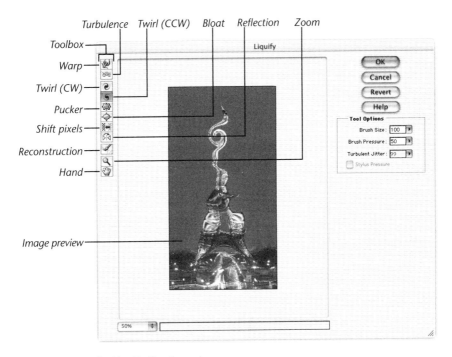

Figure 8-3 *The Liquify filter's work area*

> **AS A MATTER OF FACT** *Some filters can be memory hogs. To improve performance, try filters on a small portion of your image to see if you like the effect. Do this by first selecting a portion of your image, then apply a filter. Or you can try allocating more RAM to Elements. (See Chapter 1 for more on this.)*

There are literally dozens of ways to make your images look like artwork. We show you only a couple, but trust you'll explore others on your own. To that end, here are a few more hints to get you started: To imitate Seurat's Pointillism, try the Pointillize filter; be Picasso as Cubist with the Facet or Extrude filters; or strike out on your own with the Rough Pastels or Texturizer filters. You could even apply a combination of filters and cover the first quarter of twentieth century art all in one image.

Create an Illusion

When we think of all the great things you can do to pump up an image using filters, those that fall into the "illusion" category might very well be some of the easiest to understand and perform. "Illusion" is not one of Elements' filter categories. By illusion, we simply mean applying a filter or effect that adds a layer of reality between you and the original image, like making it look like it's underwater or behind frosted glass.

Water

Creating an illusion of water or glass is easy with Elements because there are specific filters that create the illusions. In fact, for a water illusion, you can choose from three specialized filters. To make something look like it's under water:

1. Open an image and pull the Filters palette down from the Palette Well.
2. Select the Distort category of filters from the pop-up menu in the palette.
3. Choose Ocean Ripple, Ripple, or Wave and turn off the Filter Option.
4. Click Apply.

Figure 8-4
Before ... and after the Wave filter

Glass

With the Glass filter, you can make an image look like it's behind frosted glass. But first, click the Step Backward button in the Shortcuts bar to undo the filter you applied in the previous section. Now choose the Glass filter (from the Distort category), click the Filter Option to turn it on (box should be checked), and click Apply. This time, since you enabled the Filter Option, Elements shows you the Filter Options box, where you can fine-tune the behavior of a filter. The settings here change from filter to filter, so the Filter Options you see for the Glass filter are different from the options you will see for the Wave filter.

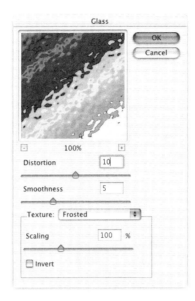

Watch the preview window as you drag the Distortion slider to the right and left; notice that the higher the number, the greater the distortion. Many Filter Option boxes use similar ideas—slider bars that correspond to aspects of the filter's effects. You can set the other options in this box in the same manner; watch the preview, stop when you see something you like, and click OK.

Add Movement

While you can't literally make an image move unless you animate it, you can employ filters to create the appearance of movement. In fact, it's so easy to do, you might wonder why we've covered it at all. We discuss it because we want to show you a few quick tricks to transform an image from not-so-exciting to how'd-you-do-that.

Blur

The Blur category of filters is helpful in camouflaging imperfections or adding a soft focus to an image. But we use a very specific Blur filter to add the appearance of movement to static images. Fittingly, it's called Motion Blur. To try it, select Blur from the pop-up categories menu in the Filters palette. Then choose Motion Blur from the palette and make sure the Filter Option is enabled so you can play with the filter settings.

Wind

The Wind filter creates the illusion of movement differently than the Motion Blur filter. Instead of blurring pixels, it adds little horizontal streaks to an image. You can find it under the Stylize category in the Filters palette. Through the Filter Option settings, you can control whether the lines move from left to right or right to left. And you can control the intensity of the effect by switching from Wind to Blast. We used the Stagger option to create the effect you see in Figure 8-6.

Figure 8-6
Before ... and
after the
Wind filter

Double Vision

We can even make an image look like it's vibrating so fast you'll think you have double-vision. Just choose Fragment from the Pixelate category of filters. And for a little extra effect, use some of the techniques we showed you in Chapter 3 to make your image look a little green around the gills.

Set the Mood with Lighting

Although we've covered a lot of ground with filters, there's plenty for you to discover on your own. But there are two especially useful filters we want to highlight before moving on, and they're both found in the Render filters category: Lens Flare and Lighting Effects. While these filters create different results, their common goal is to enable you to add realistic lighting to images.

Lens Flare

The easier of these two filters is Lens Flare. It creates the effect of a bright light, as if from a camera flash or the midday sun reflecting off a shiny object like the lens of a camera. What's more, you can apply it to a specific area of your image and control both the shape of the reflection and its intensity. To try it:

1. Open an image and pull the Filters palette down from the Palette Well.

2. Select Render from the category pop-up menu in the palette, make sure the Filter Options in the upper-left side of the palette is turned on, then choose Lens Flare and click Apply.

3. In the Filter Options settings box, enter a Brightness value (or pull the slider to the left or right) and then select a Lens Type. We chose 105mm Prime for our Lens Type and a Brightness value of 135 percent to create the illusion of a white-hot sun in the sky.

4. Click OK when you're pleased with the effect.

Figure 8-7
*We suggest
an SPF of 45.*

While the filters we've shown you are great for altering photographic images, they can also be used on files you create with Elements paint and draw tools (see Chapter 6 for a full discussion of painting). For instance, we like to use the Lens Flare filter to make an object we've drawn (like a sphere) look shiny and reflective and more three-dimensional.

Lighting Effects

The other filter we mentioned, the Lighting Effects filter, does far more than we can cover in our demonstration of it here. To be sure, you could play with this filter for days and never repeat yourself. But since our interest, for now, is in setting a mood, we'll stick to the basics and guide you through creating an effect like the one seen in Figure 8-9. To start, open an image and select Lighting Effects from the Render category of filters (make sure Filter Options is turned on), then click Apply to open the Filter Options box.

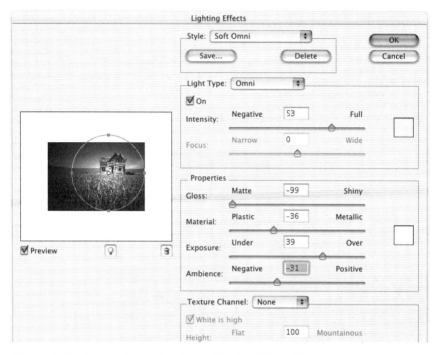

Figure 8-8 *Change the settings in the Lighting Effects Filter Option box to tweak an effect.*

In the Filter Options settings, choose Soft Omni from the pop-up Style menu and then watch the preview of your image change as you select another style from the same menu. Notice that the settings in the lower parts of the box also change. This is Elements' way of suggesting the appropriate settings for each style of lighting you choose from the pop-up menu. Now, switch back to the Soft Omni style.

While we appreciate the help Elements provides by using default values for the various settings, we want to tweak the effect a bit. So to reposition the light source, grab and drag the center circle in the image preview area. To enlarge (or shrink) the boundaries of the light, drag a handle on the outer circle. And to create a soft glow like ours, match the settings you see in Figure 8-8.

Figure 8-9
Our finished Lighting Effect creates a soft golden glow.

Create Shadows and Glows

We certainly don't want you to think that the only way to embellish an image is by using filters. They are great and powerful features, but layer styles pack a mean punch, too. They're different from filters in a couple of ways. First, while a filter can accommodate just about any image, a layer style works best on a layer that contains transparent areas (see Chapter 7). The second difference is that a layer style can always be changed from one to another (or undone), even after a file has been saved.

> **AS A MATTER OF FACT** *Layer styles save time, provide immediate satisfaction, and execute built-in effects flawlessly. Of course, as their name implies, using layer styles effectively requires an understanding of how layers work. So while you can follow our examples to get through this section, we strongly recommend that you refer to Chapter 7 of this book for a full discussion of layers. It will enrich your use of layer styles.*

Drop Shadows

To apply a drop shadow to a layer, pull the Layer Styles palette down from the Palette Well. To apply a layer style, you need a layer that contains an object or type—like we said, a layer that contains transparent areas. Open an image, create a new layer and make a rectangular selection, then fill it with a color (for help with layers, see Chapter 7; for help with a selection, see Chapter 4). Select the new layer in the

Layers palette to make it active, and find the Drop Shadow library in the pop-up
menu at the top of the Layer Styles palette.

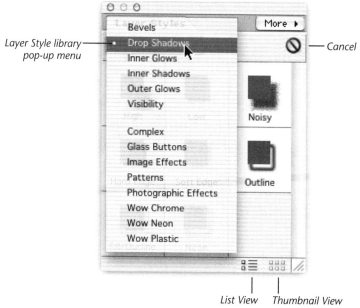

Layer Style library
pop-up menu

Cancel

List View   Thumbnail View

Figure 8-10 *The Layer Styles palette*

You'll notice that layer styles are organized, much like filters, into categories (or
libraries) that are accessed through the pop-up menu in the Layer Styles palette.
With the Drop Shadow library selected from that pop-up menu, choose the High
option from the list that appears in the palette. That's how easy it is to apply a
layer style. And Elements provides dozens of them—there are eight kinds of drop
shadows alone to choose from.

As with any layer style, we can tweak and fine-tune our drop shadow. Look for an
icon that looks like an italicized "f" inside a black circle in the Layers palette—it
indicates that a layer style is in use on that layer. Double-click it to open the Style
Settings box and drag the Shadow Distance slider bar to the right to move the
shadow away from the square.

You can also change the direction of the drop shadow. Choose any Lighting Angle
you like—this setting determines the direction of the light source—and watch your

image change as you drag the bar around the circle in the Lighting Angle section. To watch changes as you apply them to an image, make sure the Preview option in the Layer Style Settings box is turned on. And if you plan to use more than one layer style in a file, enable the Use Global Light option (so all layer styles use the same Lighting Angle) to end up with more realistic images.

AS A MATTER OF FACT *Settings in the Style Settings box are sometimes disabled (grayed out) when they don't apply to a particular layer style that's in use. For instance, if a layer doesn't use a Bevel layer style, then the option to change the bevel direction will be grayed out in the Style Settings box.*

Finally, keep in mind that layer styles correspond directly to the content boundaries of a layer. So when the boundaries of the content change, the effects change accordingly. So if you erase part of your rectangle, you'll see the effect of the layer style change to match the changing shape of your object. Go ahead and try it so you'll see what we mean.

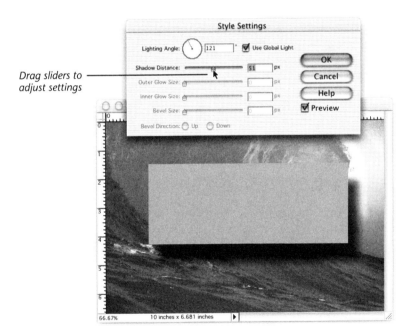

Drag sliders to adjust settings

Figure 8-11 *Adjust a layer style from the Style Settings box.*

Glows

To make an object glow, we'll use layer styles again, because there happens to be a Glow library in the Layer Styles palette. As with the previous example, we need a new layer that contains an object or type, so just add a type layer on top of the rectangle layer. If you don't know how to add type to an image, see Chapter 5 for help.

Find the Outer Glow library in the pop-up menu of the Layer Styles palette to see the different outer glows you can choose from. We like the Heavy Noisy option, so that's what we'll use—but you can pick any of them.

AS A MATTER OF FACT *If you've spent a lot of time fine-tuning a complex effect by combining styles and tweaking settings, you could lose it all at once by clicking the Cancel icon in the Layer Styles palette. Use the Step Backward button from the Shortcuts bar just above the Options bar at the top of the screen as an incremental approach to removing styles.*

Figure 8-12 *Make it glow with the Outer Glow layer style.*

You should notice a Cancel icon in the top right of the Layer Style palette (see Figure 8-10); click it to remove any and all layer styles that have been applied to a layer.

Since layer styles accumulate—add up, one on top of another—you should know that clicking the Cancel icon removes *all* applied styles at once. To remove only the last style applied, use the Step Backward button from the Shortcuts bar instead.

Although we covered only the Drop Shadows and Outer Glows categories of the layer styles, you should investigate the other kinds of shadows and glows available. The layer styles in the Inner Shadows library create shadows on the inside of your object to make it look recessed. And the Inner Glows library offers layer styles that add glow to the inner parts of your object.

Frame a Photo

Often even the most spectacular image needs a final touch—whether it's something you create from scratch in Elements or an image you import from a digital camera. Elements provides a whole set of effects for just such occasions. You can add a wood frame, a wavy frame, a drop shadow frame, or even photo corners, like you see in photo albums. We'll show you a couple of these in a moment.

But first we should explain what an effect is and how it differs from the layer styles and filters we've already discussed. Here's the key: An effect is actually a combination of layer styles and filters, sequenced and recorded for you by the good folks at Adobe. So you don't have to be a pro to get impressive results.

Photo Corners

Ever wish you had time to go through all those boxes of photos and organize them into photo albums? If you ever got around to it, you would probably use those little white photo corners to attach all the photos to clean black pages. We're too lazy for that, but we can pretend to be fastidious with the help of the Frames in the Effects palette.

To see how easy it is, try it now:

1. Open any photo and pull the Effects palette down from the Palette Well. This palette operates just like the others we've discussed in this chapter.

2. Choose the Frames library from the pop-up menu in the upper-left side of the palette.

3. Then choose the Photo Corners option.

4. Click Apply and when Elements asks if you wish to keep it, click Yes.

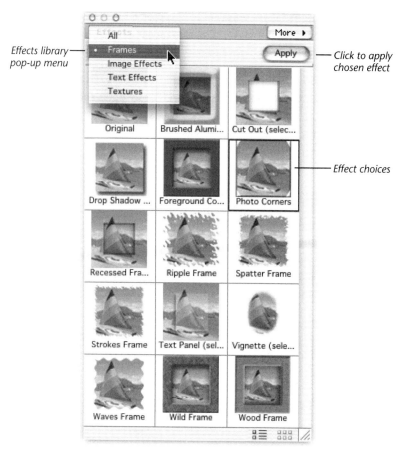

Effects library pop-up menu

Click to apply chosen effect

Effect choices

Figure 8-13   *The Effects palette*

Brushed Aluminum Frame

This time, for a more industrial look, double-click Brushed Aluminum Frame from the Effects palette and watch as Elements automatically runs through a complex set of actions—this one takes a few seconds. The bigger your image, the longer this sequence might take. And if you can see your Layers palette, you can watch as Elements works on your aluminum frame, going through a series of recorded steps. But while applying Elements' predefined effects makes impressive results easy, you can re-create them on your own with little trouble. In the next section, we'll take you through a similar series of steps to create a frame of your own—one marked with your own sense of style.

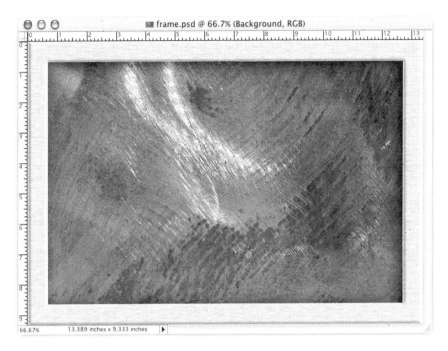

Figure 8-14 *Add an industrial look with the Brushed Aluminum Frame.*

A Frame of One's Own

Experienced users of Photoshop Elements know that any given effect might be achieved by various means. For instance, to create a vignette, you could use the Vignette effect from the Frames library in the Effects palette. Or you could use a combination of layers and fills and feathered selections. And since the effects that Elements provides are sequenced combinations of filters and functions, we can give them a run for their money working on our own. A frame, similar to the ones we previously created using the Frames effects, is the perfect opportunity to demonstrate.

Why go to all the trouble when we can just click a button on the Effects palette? Well, we're of the mind that, at some point, Elements should be about one's own personal vision. And while the preset buttons and tricks are great as tools to learn by, or ways to get something done quickly, what we cherish most is the strange alchemy that Elements facilitates. That said, let's get to it.

Open an image and be sure the Layers palette, the Effects palette, and the Layer Styles palette are all visible. Before adding a frame, let's liven up the image a bit.

Select the Image Effects library from the pop-up menu in the Effects palette and apply any option you want—we chose Blizzard. You should now see two layers in your Layers palette—your original image on the bottom, and the Blizzard effect is just above it.

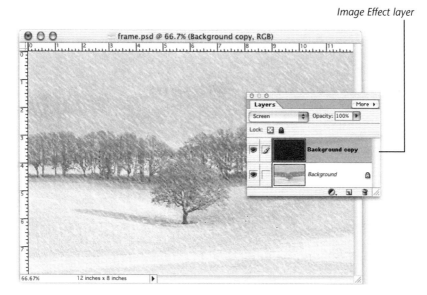

Image Effect layer

Figure 8-15   *Add some zip with Image Effects before you frame a picture.*

> **AS A MATTER OF FACT**   *The effects from the Textures library are great for creating files from scratch, like a brick wall or rosewood—these patterns and textures would take even experienced users a long time to create from scratch.*

To start the frame:

1. Select Textures from the pop-up menu in the Effects palette.

2. Choose Rosewood from the options in the palette.

3. To cut a window in the rosewood texture, to create our frame, make a selection (we used the Rectangular Marquee tool from the Toolbox) and press **DELETE**.

To add depth to our frame, find the Layer Styles palette and choose the Bevel library from the pop-up menu, then choose Simple Sharp Inner from the options. Next, select the Drop Shadow library from the same pop-up menu and select Soft Edge from those options. Now the frame is beveled and it casts a shadow, which is great, but we need to refine the effect a bit.

Figure 8-16 *The beginnings of a frame*

Double-click the little circle icon to the right of the layer's name in the Layers palette to open the (Layer) Styles Settings box. In our case, we increased both the Shadow Distance and the Bevel Size to achieve the effect you see in Figure 8-17. Remember to turn on the Preview option in the Settings box, so you can watch the effects on your image as you make adjustments to the settings.

Figure 8-17 *A finished and fine-tuned handcrafted frame*

Create Textures and Backgrounds

The creation of our frame illustrates the important principle that you can combine effects, filters, and layer styles; in fact, they work best when working together. Creating backgrounds and textures is another application in which to use them in conjunction with one another.

Why would you want to make a background or texture? Well, let's say you're building a web site and you want a subtle background to set the mood. Not a featured image, just a bit of interest. Or maybe you want to make a poster for your annual tag sale, but you want to funk it up. Perhaps you just need a change of scenery and want to load a new desktop pattern for your computer. Use the following tips and techniques as kick-starts, then create your own backgrounds and textures from scratch.

Texturize

Elements provides several filters and effects that create great textures and backgrounds on their own, like the Sandpaper and Rusted Metal effects. You'll find them in the Textures library of the Effects palette. No image or even background color is necessary for these effects. Simply start a new file, select an effect, and apply it.

1. Open a new file and make it whatever size you think you'll need.

2. Apply the Asphalt effect from the Textures library of the Effects palette. If you like that, there's no need to go further. But you can.

3. Select Paint Daubs from the Artistic category of filters.

4. In the Filter Options settings box, we entered 15 for both the Brush Size and the Sharpness values and chose the Simple Brush to create the texture you see in Figure 8-18.

5. Since the Asphalt effect used mostly black and gray, we went to **Enhance | Color | Hue/Saturation** to colorize the texture.

6. Turn on the Colorize and Preview features in the lower-left side of the Hue/Saturation box and drag the sliders around to pick a color that pleases.

7. Click OK.

Start with Color

Some effects and filters, like Lizard Skin (effect) or Texturizer (filter), work best if you start with a flat color. To try one, start a new file, select the Paint Bucket tool, choose a foreground color, and fill. Now you're ready to apply an effect or filter.

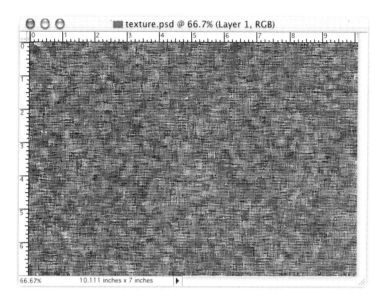

Figure 8-18 *Our colorized texture*

Select Texturizer from the Texture category in the Filters palette and pick a texture. We like the canvas texture set to 200 percent scaling and a low Relief setting (about 10).

Other filters simply do not perform well on flat color. In fact, you may not see a change at all when they're applied. These filters need a variation of color and pixels to show their stuff. So if you want to use a filter like Plastic Wrap or Motion Blur, first apply a filter like Grain or Pointillize to introduce some variation in color.

> **AS A MATTER OF FACT** *Some filters use background or foreground colors to create their effect (at the bottom of the Toolbox). The Pointillize filter is just such a filter. It uses the background color as a sort of canvas or background for the dots it creates.*

To demonstrate, start with a flat color, as we did in the previous example. Then select Maximum from the Other category of filters. Nothing happens. To introduce the variation needed, we'll apply the Pointillize filter.

But first, choose a background color that is similar (but a bit lighter) to the flat color you started with. Then apply the Pointillize filter. Now go back to the Maximum filter and enter a Radius of about 5 pixels. The results should look something like Figure 8-19.

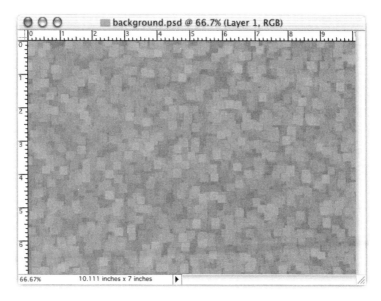

Figure 8-19 *A flat color + Pointillize filter + Maximum filter = a background*

Clouds

Elements' predefined textures are great, but some of the most amazing things happen when you combine filters and effects to create your own textures and patterns from scratch. Most of the fun is in the doing and the satisfaction that comes from success is like eating a pie you baked yourself. But like baking a pie, you need to start with some basic ingredients; the Clouds filter is our basic ingredient of choice when it comes to creating backgrounds.

Start a new file and choose a background and foreground color—it's best to choose a light color for one and a dark color for the other. Then select Clouds from the Render category in the Filters palette. This alone is good enough to use as a background, but you can do just about anything to build on this. Apply another filter to the clouds, like the Motion Blur or Crosshatch filter. Or add the Blizzard effect. You can even copy the layer, apply filters to that layer and use a blending mode to combine it with the bottom layer. See Figure 8-20 for a few ideas about how to transform clouds into interesting backgrounds.

> **AS A MATTER OF FACT** *Arrive at a texture or background you like while you're experimenting? Before you go any further, make a note of the steps that got you there for future reference.*

❶ *Clouds + Paint Daubs* ❷ *Clouds + Frosted Glass*
❸ *Clouds + Grain (Clumped) + Motion Blur*

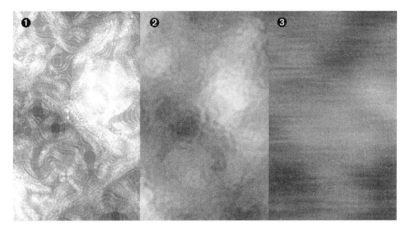

Figure 8-20 *Backgrounds from clouds*

The Clouds filter is only one of the many ingredients you can use to whip up your own background. And the handful of filters, effects, and layer styles we've shown you in this chapter aren't the only ones you can use to add interest to your images. We've only scratched the surface here, so be sure to try the ones we haven't mentioned, and don't be shy about it. Just jump right in and experiment.

Present

Here's where the rubber hits the road. It's your chance to share your personal vision and hard work with the outside world. After you've spent your valuable time and good money sprucing up and creating images, now you get to share them with others through printouts, e-mail, and the Internet.

If you've come this far, you won't be surprised to learn that Elements does much more than print images or prepare them for sharing with others. It also lets you create graphics for a personal web page, build a PDF slide show, and post a gallery of your images on the Web. Add all that to your newfound ability to whip up a more exciting newsletter, and you've got a powerful set of tools.

No matter how you plan to share your images, this chapter will help you through the basics. We'll show you just how easy it is to publish your images electronically and, if you need to see them on paper, we'll give you some tips to ensure that you get top-notch printouts.

Save Images

Anytime you're finished with an image—whether you're ready to print it, post it on the Internet, or set it aside for the time being—you first have to save it. Saving a digital image isn't as easy as stuffing it in a box (as you might a traditional photo), but it isn't rocket science either. To store a digital image, you've got to tell Elements *where* and *how* to do so. It's a little more complicated than the box method, but there are distinct advantages: No more dog-eared photos, no more faded colors, and no more boxes of unorganized photos.

Save

If you've used a computer before, you probably already know how to save a file: choose **File | Save**. You may even already know from experience that you should save files frequently to avoid lost file information if your computer crashes or the power goes out. So if you have a file open now, save and then save again, ten minutes from now. Use the Save command as a *quick save* during every work session.

First Save

But we're getting ahead of ourselves. For a moment, let's back up and take a closer look at the Save command. Launch Elements if you haven't done so already. Now, when you use the Save command for the first time on a file that's either been imported into or created with Elements, it acts as a *Save As* command. The Save As dialog box appears this first time, to ask "*Where* and *how* do you want to save this file?"

To see what we mean, choose **File | New** to start a new Elements file, set the dimensions, click OK (see Chapter 6 for help), and then save the file. Nothing happens, right? That's because you haven't done anything to the new file yet. Add something to the file (like text or a brush stroke), then try the Save command again. This time, the Save As dialog should appear (see Figure 9-1) because it's the first time you've saved that file from Elements.

Name Your File

Your first order of business in the Save As dialog box is to name the file in the field at the top of the box—it should be highlighted now. Whenever possible, make it short and sweet; don't use more than a dozen or so characters. Also, be sure not to use any spaces or weird symbols, like exclamation points or percent symbols. Names should be descriptive and nothing more; just enough to point to the contents of a file.

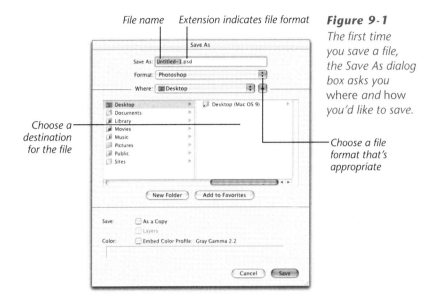

File name | Extension indicates file format

Choose a destination for the file

Choose a file format that's appropriate

Figure 9-1

The first time you save a file, the Save As dialog box asks you where and how you'd like to save.

To name your file, since it's already highlighted in the Save As field, start typing something, like "SaveDemo." See the dot (.) followed by three letters at the end of the filename? That's called the file *extension*. The fact that Elements didn't highlight the extension is really just a polite way of saying "don't mess with it." So don't. We'll talk about extensions again, but for now just remember to leave anything after the dot in a filename alone.

File Format

After you name the file, click the Format menu bar to reveal your file format options. We talked briefly about file formats in Chapter 2—and we'll have more to say about them as this chapter proceeds—but for now, choose Photoshop from the Format menu. Notice that the extension after the filename is now ".psd," which means it will be saved as a Photoshop Elements file.

Choose a Destination

You told Elements *how* to save the file by naming it and choosing a format. Now you have to tell Elements *where* to store the file. From the Where menu (Mac) or Save In (Windows), choose Desktop and look to the left side of the window in the dialog box. This shows the contents of your Desktop so you can navigate to find a place to store your image. You can even create a new folder by clicking the New Folder button.

Since this is just a demonstration (not a file we really want to keep), make sure Desktop is your choice from the Destination menu. We'll tell you about the options in the bottom section of this box shortly, but for now turn them off (unchecked) and click Save. You should now see the file you just saved on your Desktop. Now that the file has been saved once from Elements, when you open it, make changes, and use the Save command, it will act as a quick save to update the file data from the original.

Figure 9-2
Create a new folder from the Save As dialog box.

Save As

The basic Save command is a great insurance policy. But when you're done working on a file and you're ready to "publish" it, you've got to dig a little deeper.

Say you created an image in Elements that you want to share with others. The first time you saved the file, you chose the Photoshop format from the Save As dialog box (as we did in the previous section). That's smart, but now you want to send it out into the world and the .psd format isn't the smart way to do it; only people with Photoshop or Photoshop Elements can view a .psd file. Instead, you need to save another version of the file; one that's suitable for distribution. Fortunately, the Save As dialog box lets you change the format of a file at anytime. Open an image now using one of the methods you've learned in this book so we can show you how to use the Save As command. You'll want to follow along because the Save As command comes in handy on all sorts of occasions. You can use the Save As command to:

- Change the File Format
- Save a copy of a file
- Save a copy of a file to another location on your computer
- Save a flattened version of a file (more about this in Chapter 7)

With an image open, go to **File | Save As**. The familiar Save As dialog box should appear, just as it did when you used the Save command for the first time in the last section. This time, we'll show you how to dig deeper and get the greatest flexibility out of the command.

Change the File Format

Any time you open an existing Elements file, it's already stored somewhere on your computer or maybe on a CD-ROM or Zip disk (that's its destination). It already has a name and a file format. Occasionally, you might want to change one or more of these things; that's when you use the Save As command. In our case, we want the destination and filename to remain the same, so we'll leave those things alone. But we want to save the file as another file format.

Photoshop (.psd):
Use while you're
editing a file
in Elements

PDF (.pdf): Use
to compress files
you want to
share with others

TIFF (.tif): Great
format to place in
page layout
programs

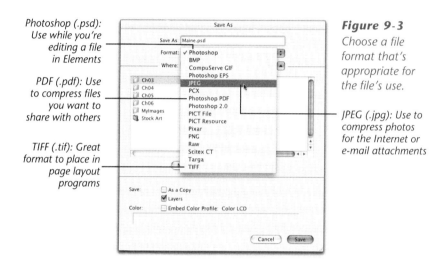

Figure 9-3
Choose a file
format that's
appropriate for
the file's use.

JPEG (.jpg): Use to
compress photos
for the Internet or
e-mail attachments

The .psd extension at the end of our file's name means that a limited number of programs can open the file—Photoshop and Elements for sure. Since we want to share our file with others, we need to change the format to something that's a little more common. We chose JPEG from the Format menu because it's perfect for sharing images with others. Then we just click Save.

Notice that the extension at the end of the filename changes to reflect the new file format. Now we have two versions of our file: one that's a Photoshop Elements file and one that's a JPEG. And because we didn't change the destination of the Save As, both files are in the same place.

That's great, but how do you know which file format to choose? Experiment a little to determine what works best for you. And in some cases, as we'll show you later in the chapter, Elements will help choose the appropriate format for you (as in attaching a file to an e-mail). But when you need to decide for yourself, refer to the following for a rundown of the most common and useful file formats found in the Format menu of the Save As dialog box:

Photoshop (.psd)   This is the native format for Photoshop Elements, therefore the number of programs that can open these files is limited. While some file formats compress and flatten files, the .psd format leaves layers and all other information intact. For example, some other formats cannot save layers, but the .psd format can. This is why, when you start a file, whether it's one you create in Elements or import for editing, it's a good idea to save it as a Photoshop file and use that format throughout the editing process.

TIFF (.tif)   The pros favor the TIFF format for its all-purpose nature and pleasant disposition. TIFF files get along well with others, whether on a PC or on a Mac, which is why they are great for use in a page layout programs (or even Word); and they are especially good for high-resolution images. In fact, the images you see in this book are TIFFs because it's a good choice for commercially printed materials.

JPEG (.jpg)   JPEG files result in dramatically smaller file sizes through compression of data, so it's good to use for photos that will be posted on the Web. The compressed files are also perfect for e-mail attachments, since they travel quickly and many programs can open them.

PDF (.pdf)   PDF is another great choice when you want to send a file as an e-mail attachment because it compresses the data (resulting in a smaller file size) and it's readable by anyone who has the *free* Adobe program called Acrobat Reader. And because this format embeds fonts, it's especially useful for files that contain type—the type will display properly even if the recipient doesn't have the font.

AS A MATTER OF FACT   *You should find a copy of Adobe Acrobat Reader on the Photoshop Elements install CD-ROM; anyone can download this free software from the Adobe web site: www.adobe.com/products/acrobat/readstep2.html.*

Print

After you save an image, the first thing you might want to do is print it. On the one hand, printing is as simple as making sure your printer is connected to your computer and working properly. Once you do, just open the image and go to **File | Print**. However, without making a few preliminary adjustments, there's no guarantee the printed piece will be worth the ink used to print it. So it's a good idea to start with the Print Preview.

Print Preview

If your printer is connected and turned on, go ahead and launch Elements, open an image you want to print, and choose **File | Print Preview**. This should be your first step to printing—a sort of pit stop before the real action starts. The Print Preview dialog box provides a sneak peek at the printed page.

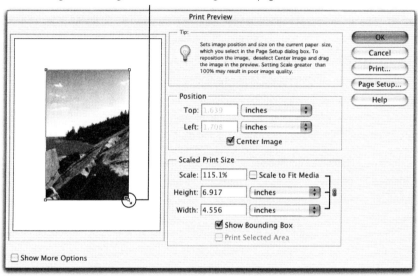

With the Show Bounding Box option enabled, you can grab and drag here to scale an image on the page

Figure 9-4 *The Print Preview dialog box provides an important overview of your printing options.*

AS A MATTER OF FACT *Be sure to consult the Tip portion of the Print Preview dialog box for great advice and general guidance.*

Page Setup

The first thing to check is the Page Setup, so click the Page Setup button now. Click the Format For menu and select your printer; if you don't see the name of your printer here, check your printer's manual to make sure you have it hooked up correctly. After you choose your printer from the Format For menu, select a paper size from the Paper Size menu, choose an orientation, and click OK to return to the Print Preview dialog box.

Scale

To center your image on the page, make sure the Center Image box (in the top section of the dialog box) is checked. You have two options when it comes to sizing your image: You can enter values for the Scaled Print Size settings or you can click and drag the corners of the bounding box (make sure Show Bounding Box is checked) in the preview window (see Figure 9-4). If you're enlarging the image on the page, be sure to consult the next section for some tips. Size the image on the page and click Print when you like what you see.

> **AS A MATTER OF FACT** *Scaling an image in the Print Preview dialog box does not affect the actual image file, only the printout.*

Resolution

Print Preview helps ensure that you're truly ready to print before you waste ink and paper. That's why we recommend using it every time. But there's only so much Print Preview can do. There are other contingencies you'll have to prepare for on your own, foremost among these is addressing the issue of image size and resolution.

We discussed resolution in Chapter 2, but to recap: Resolution is the measurement of the density of pixels in an image and it affects the overall quality of an image. For purposes of printing, keep in mind that the higher the resolution, the better the quality of your image—although there's no need to go above 300–pixels-per-inch. See Chapter 2 for recommendations on what resolution to use for what purpose. The rule of thumb for printing good quality images to an ink-jet printer is 180-pixels-per-inch for good-quality black-and-white images and about 300-pixels-per-inch for good-quality color images.

> **AS A MATTER OF FACT** *Just remember that enlarging an image on the page can degrade the quality of your printout; reducing the size isn't a problem. If you need an image to be bigger, you might be better off re-creating the image at a larger size.*

Paper

Another factor that can greatly influence the quality of your printouts is the paper. There are a lot of high-quality ink-jet papers out there: matte, glossy, photo quality, general use, there's even paper that looks like artist canvas. Be sure to choose an appropriate paper for your job. For instance, if you want to print extremely high-quality photographs, a nice photo-quality paper will yield much better results than plain-vanilla copy paper.

It's a good idea to keep some inexpensive paper around for test runs. When you print photos, print the first one on cheap paper to see if everything works properly. If it comes out OK, then you know it's safe to print the image on the pricey paper. Specialty papers can cost a small fortune, so plan ahead and do some test runs on cheap paper so you don't flush money down the drain.

For general use, any old printer and ink will do fine, although the inks will fade in time. But if you plan to print a lot of photos—and you want them to last a long time—investigate your options for special photo ink-jet printers, archival inks, and paper. The industry has made great strides in recent years to tackle the problem of fading inks, and you don't have to spend loads of cash to get more permanent images. For more on the permanence of inkjet images, visit www.wilhelm-research.com for the latest research and technology.

Save Paper

If you plan to print multiple copies of an image, you can save paper and save yourself time by using one of the Print Layout features in Elements. Each provides a simple way to save paper by printing multiple images on a single page.

Picture Package

If you want to print ten copies of a wallet size photo to pass around the office, you could meticulously copy and paste the image over and over to create one file that contains multiple copies of the image and then print it. Or, you could print the image ten times and waste a whole lot of paper. But the best option is to try Elements' handy Picture Package feature (see Figure 9-5). You don't have to have an image open, just make sure Elements is running and choose **File | Print Layouts | Picture Package**.

The Picture Package dialog box appears. First select 8x10 inches from the Page Size menu; this will keep your layout inside the margins of standard letter size paper. Now you can choose a layout from the Layout menu. For instance, we chose (1) 5x7 (2) 3.5x5. Now you should see a preview of the layout you just chose, on the right.

Just below the Layout menu, you should see the Resolution field. For a good printout of a color image on a decent ink-jet printer, 300-pixels-per-inch should be your high-end benchmark value. But, unfortunately, it's not that simple. You have to know the image you're dealing with to get good results. No matter what you specify as the Resolution in the Picture Package dialog box, your printout will only be as good as the resolution in the original Elements file.

Figure 9-5 *The Picture Package command is a great way to set up a paper-saving layout.*

> **AS A MATTER OF FACT** *If you want to customize your layout, double-click on an image in the preview, then tell Elements which image to use as a replacement.*

The last thing to set up in the Document section is the color of your printout. Assuming you want color printouts from a color printer, click the Mode menu and choose RGB Color. Then make sure the Flatten All Layers box is checked. And if you want labels added to your layout, use the settings in the Label section of the dialog box. We chose None from the Content menu here so no labels will be added to our layout. When you're pleased with the package preview, click OK and Elements will create a picture package that you can save and/or print.

Contact Sheet

Another handy way to save paper (and create a physical archive of your images) is to print a contact sheet, which is a printed set of thumbnail images that you can use as reference. For example, you can print a set of contact sheets, broken down by storage folders, to use later as a reference and file inventory. If you need to know what the name of such-and-such image is, just flip through your contact sheets to find it.

Go to **File | Print Layouts | Contact Sheet**. In the Contact Sheet dialog box, you must first choose a Source Folder—this is where organization of your images into various folders can really pay off. If you haven't organized your files into folders, you'll need to do that first, then go back to the Contact Sheet command.

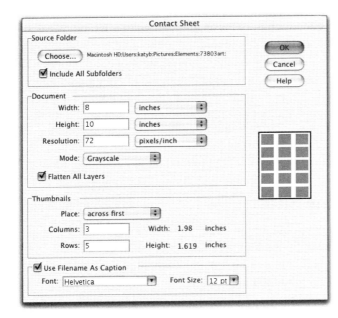

Figure 9-6
The Contact Sheet option is perfect if you want a hard copy index of your digital photos.

Next, specify the page size and how you'd like your thumbnails arranged. You can even enable the Use Filename As Caption option so you'll see the filename for each thumbnail on the contact sheet. After you've specified a source folder and selected your settings, click OK. Then watch as Elements does the rest. When the contact sheet is generated, you can then save and/or print it.

> **AS A MATTER OF FACT** *Elements will include thumbnails of all images in the Source folder, even if it takes multiple contact sheets to finish the job.*

E-mail an Image

Ever been tortured by a friend who owns a digital camera? They send pictures attached to e-mails that take hours to download. Do them a favor and set a good example by sending images that are always sized and saved to prevent e-mail bottlenecks. You'll get all the praise, while Elements does all the work.

1. Open an image and go to **File | Attach to E-mail**.

2. If your file isn't already a JPEG (the appropriate file format for an e-mail attachment), Elements will ask if you'd like it converted; always click the Auto Convert button.

3. A new e-mail message opens with the image attached to it; all you have to do is address the message and add your note.

4. Send it.

> **AS A MATTER OF FACT** Don't worry. When Elements automatically converted your image to a JPEG it didn't alter the original image; it created a copy of the image to send.

Present a Slide Show

If you're not quite ready to post your images on the Internet, but you'd like to present your images electronically, try the PDF Slideshow feature that's built into Elements. It's fully automated and a snap to set up. Simply choose **File | Automations Tools | PDF Slideshow**.

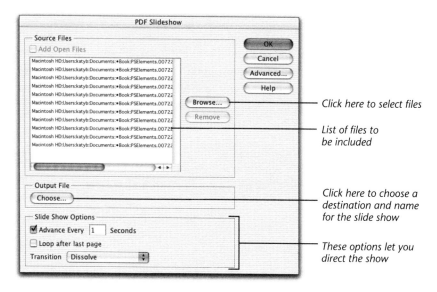

Figure 9-7   Set up your slide show in the PDF Slideshow dialog box.

Select Images

In the PDF Slideshow dialog box, click the Browse button to find the images you want to include in the slide show. Each time you select an image, it's included in the Source Files window of the dialog box. If you change your mind about an image, just select it from this list and click Remove. You can also rearrange the order of images from the Source Files list—just select and drag the file up or down in the list. Go ahead and choose ten or so images (you can include more than that if you like). Once you're satisfied with the images in the show (and their order), click Choose to name your file and pick a destination for the saved slide show file.

Direct Your Show

See the Slide Show Options portions of the dialog box? These options allow you to direct your show so you can specify how many seconds each image will stay on screen, make the show continuously play by activating the Loop option, and control the transitions between slides. With all the options set, click OK and watch Elements go to work; it will notify you when the slide show is complete.

View Your Slide Show

To effectively view the slide show, you must have Adobe Reader version 5.0 (or later)—if you don't already have it, copy it from the Elements 2.0 CD-ROM to your computer's hard drive. Now, double-click the slide show file and Acrobat will launch to play your slide show.

AS A MATTER OF FACT   *If the slide show works, and the file size is less than 1MB or so, you can share the show with others via e-mail. Just attach the document to an e-mail and send it to friend. But don't forget to tell them that they'll need Acrobat Reader to view the show.*

Prepare an Image for the Web

Typically, if you save an image as a JPEG with a resolution of 72-pixels-per-inch, it's more or less ready for the Web. It doesn't mean, however, that it's perfect. In general, while large files result in a better-looking image, they take longer to load in an Internet browser. So, in the end, posting images on the Web is a balancing act of image quality and file size.

If you've surfed the Internet, you've probably run across a page that seems to take forever to load—it's often caused by improper image optimization. The site's creators didn't balance their options carefully. If you don't want to try the patience of others, you need to know how to optimize your image for the Web, and if you choose the Save for Web command, Elements will lend a hand.

Save for Web

The best way to share your images with the widest audience is to display them on a web page. If you have Internet access and an e-mail account, your provider probably offers free space on their server for a personal web page. There are also a number of online sources that offer free web hosting. Sometimes they even provide web page templates that make creating a personal web site a breeze.

But if you want to include images on your web page, you have to *optimize* (or compress) them first. To do that, open an image and go to **File | Save for Web**. The first thing you notice in the Save for Web dialog box are the side-by-side previews of your image. The left side displays the original image, and the right side displays how the image will look after it's been optimized. Then, along the right side of the dialog box, you should notice the settings that control the optimization of an image.

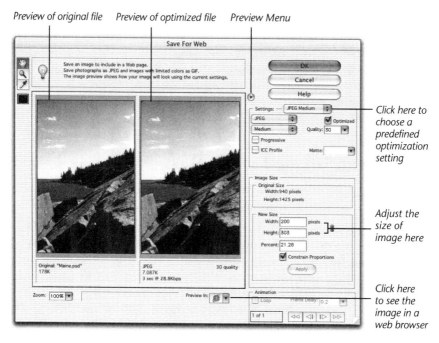

Preview of original file   *Preview of optimized file*   *Preview Menu*

Click here to choose a predefined optimization setting

Adjust the size of image here

Click here to see the image in a web browser

Figure 9-8 *The Save for Web dialog box makes it easy to optimize files for the Web.*

Use a Predefined Setting

The best place to start is with the predefined optimization settings found in the menu just under the Help button. Click it to see the options now. There's a lot to consider here, but just keep this general rule in mind: Photographs or images with lots of colors and shading should be optimized as JPEGs, and images that contain large areas of flat color and crisp details should be optimized as GIFs. Our image is a photograph, so we chose JPEG Medium as a starting point.

Fine-Tune the Settings

When you choose a predefined optimization setting, Elements automatically sets the options in the Settings portion of the dialog box for you. For the most part, you can trust these. But don't assume that takes care of everything; there are a few things you should check. And since we can't walk you through every detail in the Save for Web dialog box, we suggest you use the Help feature that Elements provides, and then follow the general guidelines we provide in the following sections.

Image Size

If you know what size you want your image to be on the web page, the New Size section is where you take care of that. It's important to remember that the physical size of an image affects file size, which affects load time. In light of this, it's a good practice to make sure the New Size reflects the actual size you will use on the web page—no bigger, no smaller. Each time you change the size here, click Apply to see how the change affects the optimization (watch the preview and the information below the preview).

Optimization Information

Even if the preview of your optimized image looks good, it's not proof that everything is as it should be. The real proof is in the information below the preview, so don't overlook it. The Optimization Information here will tell you the file format that will be used to save the image, its file size, and most important, an estimate of the time it will take an Internet browser to load the image.

That last bit of information is what optimization is all about; it's the balancing act part of the equation. As a general rule, you want the shortest possible download time, without sacrificing too much image quality. The best rule of thumb here is to use your own instincts. That is, think about how long you'd wait to see an image load into an Internet browser. We think 4 to 8 seconds is a good target, so if the estimate is more than that, you may need to make further adjustments in the optimization settings.

Figure 9-9
Select 28.8Kbps
Modem from the
Preview Menu.

Elements estimate here is directly affected by the choice made from Preview Menu (see Figure 9-8). Click on it now and make sure the setting for modem speed is 28.8Kbps Modem. This means that Elements will use this modem speed to come up with an estimated load time. You could change the modem speed, but 28.8Kbps is safe for a broad base of Internet users, so it's what we suggest.

Create a Photo Gallery

The Save for Web command assumes that you know how to post images on the Web once they've been optimized. First, they have to be placed into an html file, then the html file has to be uploaded to a web server. You can contact your Internet service provider for instructions on how to upload files to your personal web space, so that's no problem. But creating an html file is another matter. Perhaps you don't know what html is; even that's not a problem. Elements take care of all of this html stuff for you, so it's painless.

Gather Images

Let's say you want to post a series of photos from your wedding on a web site. Elements can do all of this for you with one command. All you have to do is tell it what images you want to include and then pick from a handful of predefined layouts. Piece of cake.

If you have image files scattered all over your hard drive, you should organize them first. All you need is a folder that contains image files. You could even use the File Browser (see Chapter 2) to organize your images; create a folder that contains only the images you want to display in your web gallery. Once you've done that, choose **File | Create Web Photo Gallery** to open the Web Photo Gallery dialog box.

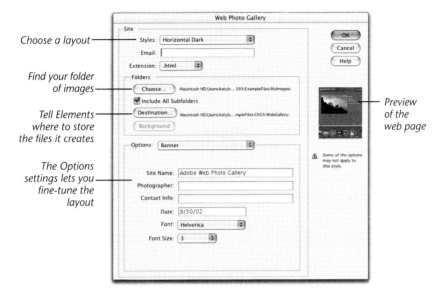

Choose a layout

Find your folder of images

Tell Elements where to store the files it creates

The Options settings lets you fine-tune the layout

Preview of the web page

Figure 9-10 *The Create Web Photo Gallery command makes posting images on the Web painless.*

Setup

Choose a design template from the Styles menu. As you make a choice from this menu, you'll see a preview of the design on the right side of the dialog box. Choose one that suits your taste. Once you've settled on a template, you can enter your e-mail address in the Email field, if you want it to display in the gallery (not all styles give you this option). Then choose .html from the Extension menu.

Choose an Image Folder

To show Elements which images to include in the gallery, click the Choose button. From the dialog box that appears, navigate to the appropriate folder on your hard drive (the one containing the images you'd like to display) and, if the folder contains subfolders full of images, check the Include All Subfolders checkbox. When you've located the appropriate folder(s), click Choose.

Choose a Destination

Now you have to show Elements where to put all the stuff it creates for you—the compressed images and the html file it generates. Click the Destination button to open the destination dialog box. Select Desktop from the From menu at the top and click the New Folder button, name the folder something like "webgallery1," then click Create. Back in the destination location dialog box, make sure you select the folder you just created and then click Choose.

Choose Options

Take a look at the bottom portion of the Web Photo Gallery dialog box. This is where you can control the way images are displayed in the gallery. You can also choose to include information like captions or copyright notices. Each option from the menu has its own set of inputs in the area below the menu. Click the Options menu to see your choices and then refer to the following sections for a brief rundown on the setup:

Figure 9-11
The Options menu

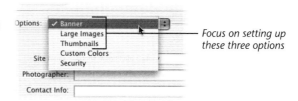

— *Focus on setting up these three options*

Banner

Choose Banner from the Options menu to set up a title for your gallery and type something in the Site Name field. What you put here will display in the Internet browser's Title bar, so choose something descriptive, like Nathaniel and Sophia's Wedding. If you want, you can also enter the name of the photographer (if you want to give credit), the date, and choose some font options. The default settings here are usually adequate.

Choose Image Size

A web gallery usually starts by displaying a group of thumbnails—one for each image in the gallery. Click on a thumbnail and you get to see a larger version of the image. This is the way Elements will build your gallery. But first, you have to tell Elements how you'd like to display each version of the image: Large Images and Thumbnails.

Select Large Images from the Options menu now. We suggest that you first try the default settings for this option; they should be fine for general use. Of course, if you don't like the results—say images end up being smaller onscreen than you'd like; or it takes too long to load into the browser—you can always redo the file and revisit these settings.

To tell Elements how to display the thumbnails of your images, select Thumbnails from the Options menu. Again, try the default settings for this option and revisit them if you need to. Go ahead and skip the Color and Security options for now, and click OK.

Make Elements Work

Once you click OK, you can sit back and watch Elements do all the heavy lifting. It opens each image and compresses, resizes, and saves them to meet the Options settings you specified. Then it generates the html code and places everything together in the destination folder you created. Once it's finished, it launches your web browser to show you how the gallery will look on the Internet. All of this could take a few minutes if you've included lots of images, so sit tight.

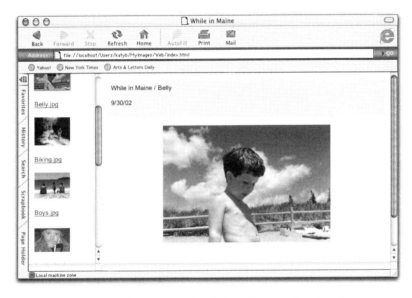

Figure 9-12   *Elements shows you a simulation of your web gallery in an Internet browser.*

When it's finished, you'll see what the gallery will look like when it's posted on the Internet. But remember, it's only a simulation. To actually post the gallery, you'll have to do a little homework: Contact your ISP (Internet service provider), your web host, or an Internet-savvy friend to find out how to post your web gallery online.

Index

A

Add To Selection button, 70

Adjust Backlighting command, 47-48

Adjustment Layer, color adjustments, 54-55

Adobe Acrobat Reader, 172, 179

Adobe Gamma utility, 43-44

Adobe web site, 20

alignment options, type, 89

angle and roundness option, Brush tool, 114

Angled Strokes filter, 145-146

anti-aliasing
  Lasso tool, 68
  Magnetic Lasso tool, 76
  type, 88-89

Area field, brush strokes, 119

Arrange commands, 130

artistic filters, 144

Auto Color Correct, 53

Auto Contrast command, 51

Auto Convert button, 178

Auto Levels command
  color-cast created by, 48
  improving tonal range with, 51

B

background color
  selecting, 103
  settings, 14

background layers
  Clouds filter and, 164-165
  combining images and, 122-123
  stacking order of, 129

backlighting adjustments, 47-48

banner option, Web Photo Gallery, 184

base layers, 97, 133

beveled type

    adding shadows to, 96

    creating, 95

bitmap images, 22-23, 93

black and white photos, colorizing, 117-118

blank canvases, 102

Blast filter, 150

blending colors, 115-117

blending modes, layers, 130-131

Blur category, of filters, 149

Blur tool, 61-62

Browse option, Welcome Screen, 2

browsing images, 34-36

    customizing File Browser, 36

    with File Browser, 34-35

    finding files, 35

Brush Strokes filters, 144, 146

Brush tool

    angle and roundness option, 114

    colorizing images and, 117-118

    fade options, 114, 116

    hardness option, 114

    opacity options, 116

    Options bar, 107-109

    scatter option, 114

    size options, 113

    spacing options, 114

Brushed Aluminum frame, 158-159

brushes

    customizing, 113-115

    Default Brush library, 108

    options, 107-109

    pressure settings, 146

    selecting, 107

    specialty, 108

    tips, 108

Brushes pop-up palette, 107-109

C

cameras. *See* digital cameras

Canvas Size, 29-30

canvases

    blank, 102

    cleaning with Eraser tool, 109

    filling with paint, 110-112

Clone Stamp tool, 57-59

Clouds filter, 164

color-cast

    created by Auto Levels command, 48

    removing, 51

Color-Cast command, 51

color depth setting, monitors, 42-43

Color field, 103

color jitter option, Brush tool, 114

color modes, 27-29

Color Picker

    changing layer colors, 124

    illustration of, 104

    opening, 90

    specifying paint color with, 103-104

color sliders, 103

color variations

    Color Variations dialog box, 52-53

    filters and, 162-163

colors

    adding with paint tools, 106-107

    Adjustment Layer, 54-55

    balance, 53

    blending, 115-117

    colorizing an image, 117-118

    enhancements, 53-54

    of layers, 124

    libraries, 106-107

    monitor calibration, 42-44

    type, 90

    variability of, 42

combined palettes, 11-12

commands. *See* menu commands

Common Issues option, Welcome Screen, 2

complex selections, 75-79

Connect to Camera or Scanner option, 2, 37

Contact Sheet dialog box, 176-177

Contract command, selection modification, 80

contrast, 47-51

    adjustments, 48

    Auto Contrast command, 51

    Edge contrast, 77

    Levels command, 49-51

    light/dark balance, 47

copies, incorporating into images, 81-82

Copy command, 72

cover up tools, 57-59

    Clone Stamp tool, 57-59

    Smudge tool, 57

creation tools, 13

Crop tool, 64-66

    adjusting crop, 65-66

    opening, 64

    Shield option, 65

Custom Shape tool, 123

D

Default Brush library, 108

defragmentation, 18

depth options, type, 95-96

digital cameras

    connecting to, 2

    guide to use of, 37

    importing photos from, 37-38

digital video cameras, 39-40

disk defragmentation, 18

Distort command, 93

Distort filters, 148

docked palettes, 12

double-vision effect, 150

dragging layers, 130, 134-135

drop shadows, 96, 153-155

duplicating layers, 134

E

Edge contrast, Magnetic Lasso tool, 77

Edit menu

    Copy and Paste commands, 72

    general commands, 8

editing

    type, 87

    undo/redo limits for, 11

effects
  combining with filters and
    styles, 162
  frames, 157-161
  glow, 156-157
  lighting, 150-153
  movement, 149-150
  shadows, 153-155
  Warp, 91, 91-93, 146
  waves, 91-93
Effects palette
  Frames library, 157
  Rusted Metal option, 97
  Textures library, 160, 162
Elliptical Marquee tool, 66, 70
e-mailing images, 177-178
embellishing images, 143-165
  filters, 144-145
  frame effects, 157-161
  glow effects, 156-157
  illusions, 148-149
  impressionist style, 145-146
  lighting effects, 150-153
  movement effects, 149-150
  shadow effects, 153-155
  surrealist style, 146-147
  textures and backgrounds, 162-165
Enhance color, 53-54
EPS file format, 32-33
Eraser tool, 109
Exit option, Welcome Screen, 3
Expand command, selection
  modification, 80
extensions, filename, 169

Extrude filter, 147
Eye icon, layer visibility, 126
Eyedropper tool, 106

F

Facet filter, 147
fade options, Brush tool, 114, 116
feather option
  Lasso tool, 68
  Magnetic Lasso tool, 76
File Browser
  customizing, 36
  finding files, 35
  organizing files, 36-37
  overview of, 34-35
  renaming files, 36
file formats
  changing, 170-172
  images, 32
  options, 169
File menu
  commands, 8
  opening images from, 4
filename extensions, 169
files
  finding, 35
  organizing, 36-37
  renaming, 36
  size and memory requirements, 136
Fill Flash command, 47
fill options, type, 97-100
Filter Options settings, 149
filters, 144-153

Angled Strokes, 145-146

artistic, 144

Blast, 150

blur category, 61-62, 149

Brush Strokes, 144, 146

combining with styles and effects, 162

contrasted with layer styles, 153

Distort, 148

Extrude, 147

Facet, 147

Glass, 148

Lens Flare, 150-151

Lighting Effects, 151-152

Liquify, 146-147

Motion Blur, 149

movement effects, 149-150

Ocean Ripple, 148

Options settings, 149

overview of, 144-145

Paint Daubs, 146

Palette Knife, 146

Pointillize, 147, 163-164

RAM use by, 147

render category, 151-152, 164

Rough Pastel, 147

Smudge Stick, 146

Texturizer, 147, 162-163

Unsharp Mask, 59-60

using color variations with, 162-163

wave effects, 148

wind effects, 149-150

Filters palette, 144-145

fine-tuning tools, 59

blur filters, 61-62

Sharpen tool, 60-61

Unsharp Mask filter, 59-60

Finger Painting option, 116

flattening layers, 137-138

flaws, retouching, 56-59

cover ups, 57-58

red eye, 56-57

Flip command, 8, 73

fonts, 88

foreground color

selecting, 103

settings, 14

formats

file formats, 32-34

importing images, 40

video still images, 39

formatting type, 87

frame effects, 157-161

Brushed Aluminum frame, 158-159

custom frames, 159-161

photo corners, 157

Frames library, 157

Free Transform, type, 93

Frequency setting, Magnetic Lasso tool, 77

G

Glass filter, 148

glow effects, 156-157

Glow library, 156

gradient fills, 110-111, 124

Grayscale mode, 118

Grid, turning on/off, 7

grouping layers, 133-134

Grow command, 79

H

halo of pixels, removing, 81-82

handles, scaling images with, 73

hardness option, Brush tool, 114

help

    Adobe web site, 20

    Help menu, 20

    Hints palette, 19-20

Hints palette, 19-20

Horizontal Type tool, 86, 90

HSB color, 104

html files, 182

Hue/Saturation, color enhancements,
53-54

I

illusions, 148-149. *See also* effects

Image Area, of Image Window, 5

Image Window, 4-6

    functions of, 4-5

    Image Area of, 5

    magnifying images, 15-16

    navigating Image Area, 16-17

    resizing, 7

    Rulers and Grid, 7

    Status bar, 6

    Title bar, 5

images, 21-40

    adjusting with Quick Fix window,
45-46

    browsing, 34-36

    Canvas Size and, 29-30

    color modes, 27-29

    colorizing, 117-118

    combining. *See* layers

    commands, 8

    embellishing. *See* embellishing
images

    file formats, 32

    flipping, 8

    importing. *See* importing images

    magnifying, 15-16

    opening, 4, 31-34

    printing. *See* printing images

    resampling, 25

    resizing, 24-25

    resolution and, 174

    rotating, 8-9

    saving. *See* saving images

    sharing. *See* sharing images

    size limitations, 181, 184-185

    size vs. resolution, 26-27

    types of, 22-23

Import command, 37-38

    importing photos, 37

    importing scanned images, 38

importing images, 37-40

    photos, 37-38

    scanned images, 37-38

    TWAIN interface and, 39

video stills, 39-40

WIA utility for, 39

Impressionist Brush, 118

impressionist style, 145-146

insertion point, type, 87

inverse selections, 83-84

irregular shapes, selecting, 67-70

J

JPEG (.jpg) file format

emailing images and, 178

overview of, 172

K

keyboard shortcuts, 9

L

Lasso tools

anti-aliasing, 68

applying, 68-69

Feather option, 68

illustration of, 67

Magnetic Lasso, 75-76

Polygonal Lasso, 71-72

selection mode, 68

layer styles

categories of, 154

contrasted with filters, 153

drop shadows, 96, 153-155

Emboss Layer Style, 95

glow, 156

patterns, 98

Wow Plastic Layer Styles, 96

Layer Styles palette, 98, 154, 156

layers, 121-141

adding shapes, 123

adding type, 124-125

backgrounds, 122-123

blending images and, 130-131

building, 122

cleaning up, 135-136

colors, 124

deleting, 136

dragging, 134-135

duplicating, 134

flattening, 137-138

grouping, 97, 133-134

image transparency, 131-132

linking, 130

locking, 136

masking images, 132-133

merging, 137

moving, 128

ordering, 130

panoramas and, 138-141

reordering, 129

simplifying, 124

typographic, 87

Layers palette

docking palettes and, 12

functions of, 125-127

illustration of, 126

Lens Flare filter, 150-151

Levels command, 49-51

libraries

    color, 104-105

    default brushes, 108

    drop shadows, 154

    frames, 157

    glow, 156

    textures, 160, 162

lighting adjustments, 47-48

    Adjust Backlighting command, 48

    Fill Flash command, 47-48

Lighting Angles, 154-155

lighting effects, 150-153

Lighting Effects filter, 151-152

linking layers, 127, 130

Liquify filter, 146-147

List View icon, Filters palette, 145

Lizard Skin effect, 162

Lock All check box, 136

Lock Transparency check box, 132-133

locking layers, 136

M

Magic Wand tool

    applying, 82-83

    illustration of, 67

Magnetic Lasso tool

    applying, 77-79

    complex selections with, 75-76

    feather and anti-aliasing options, 76

    selection mode, 76

    settings, 76

    width, edge contrast, and
        frequency, 76-77

magnifying images, 15-16

    techniques for, 15

    Zoom tool, 15-16

Marquees

    Elliptical Marquee tool, 66

    illustration of, 67

    Regular Marquee tool, 66-67

masks, 132-133

    functions of, 132

    Lock Transparency check box and,
        132-133

memory

    allocating use of, 18

    file size and, 136

    filters use of, 147

Menu bar

    commands on, 7-8

    illustration of, 4

menu commands, 7-9

    Arrange, 130

    Auto Contrast, 51

    Color-Cast, 51

    Contract, 80

    Copy, 72

    Distort, 93

    Expand, 80

    Fill Flash, 47

    Flip, 8, 73

    Grow, 79

    Import, 37-38

    Levels, 49-51

    overview of, 7

    Paste, 72

    Perspective, 94

Print, 172-173

Print Preview, 173-175

Rotate, 8, 74

Save, 168

Save As, 170

Scale, 73

Shortcuts bar, 9

Similar, 80

Skew, 93

Smooth, 80-81

Straighten and Crop Image, 46

types of menus and, 8

merging layers, 137

miscellaneous tools, 14

modem speed, 182

modifying selections, 79-81

Expand or Contract commands, 80

Grow command, 79

Similar command, 80

Smooth command, 80-81

monitor calibration, 42-44

Motion Blur filter, 149

Move tool

moving layers, 128

moving selections, 74-75

moving type, 90-91

movement effects, 149-150

N

naming files, 168-169

navigating Image Area, 16-17

Navigator palette, 16-17

New option, Welcome Screen, 2

O

Ocean Ripple filter, 148

Opacity options, Brush tool, 116

Opacity settings, layers, 132

Open dialog box, 4

opening images, 31-34

EPS files, 32-33

files formats and, 32

PDF files, 33

Photo CD files, 33-34

recent images, 31

Optimization settings, Save for Web, 181

Options bar

Brush tool, 107-109

illustration of, 4

Lasso tool, 68

setting tool options, 14-15

Tolerance settings, 79

Type tools, 88

Options menu, Web Photo Gallery, 184

orientation, of type, 90

Outer Glow layer style, 156-157

P

Page Setup, Print Preview, 173

Paint Bucket tool, 111-113

Paint Daubs filter, 146

paint tools, 101-119

adding color, 106-107

blank canvas, creating, 102

blending colors, 135-137

brush customization, 133-135

brush options, 127-129

brush selection, 127

Color Picker, 103-104

colorizing an image, 137-138

Eraser tool, 129

foreground/background color, 103

Gradient tool, 130-131

Paint Bucket tool, 131-133

Swatches palette, 104-106

turning photos into paintings,
    138-139

Paintbrush icon, layers, 126-127

paintbrushes. *See* brushes

paintings, turning photos into,
    118-119

Palette Knife filter, 146

Palette Well, 10-12

    combining palettes, 11-12

    docking palettes, 12

    illustration of, 4

    overview of, 10

    viewing palettes, 10-11

palettes

    Brushes pop-up, 107-109

    combining, 11-12

    defined, 10

    docking, 12

    Effects, 97, 157, 160, 162

    Filters, 144-145

    Hints, 19-20

    Layer Styles, 98, 154, 156

    Layers, 12, 125-127

    Navigator, 16-17

    resizing, 10

Swatches, 104-107

Undo History, 10-12

    viewing, 10-11

panoramas, 138-141

paper

    quality, 174-175

    saving, 175-177

Paste command, 72

pattern fills, 124

Patterns library, 98

PDF (.pdf) file format, 33, 172

PDF Slideshow feature, 178-179

    image selection, 178

    Loop option, 179

    viewing, 179

performance preferences, 17-18

Perspective command, 94

Photo CD file format, 33-34

photo corners, 156-157

Photo Gallery. *See* Web Photo Gallery

photographs

    stock photographs, 122

    turning into paintings, 118-119

Photomerge dialog box, 140-141

Photoshop (.psd) file format

    filenames and, 169

    overview of, 172

    saving imported images in, 40

Picture Package feature, 175-176

pixels

    adding to selections, 70

    removing from selections, 71-72

    removing halo of, 81-82

resolution and, 174

selection modification and, 79-80

selection tools and, 13

point sizes, type, 88

Pointillize filter, 147, 163-164

Polygonal Lasso tool, 71-72

Preferences, 17-18

Print command, 172-173

Print Preview command, 173

Page Setup, 173

paper quality, 174-175

resolution, 174

Scaled Print Size settings, 174

printing images, 172-177

Contact Sheet dialog box, 176-177

Page Setup, 173

paper quality, 174-175

Picture Package, 175-176

Print command, 172, 172-173

Print Preview command, 173

resolution and, 174

Scaled Print Size settings, 173

.psd format. *See* Photoshop (.psd)
file format

Q

Quick Fix window, 45-46

R

random access memory (RAM)

filters use of, 147

requirements for, 17-18

Red Eye Brush, 56-57

Regular Marquee tool, 66-67

Render category, of filters, 151-152, 164

resampling images, 25

resizing

Image Window, 7

images, 24-25

type, 88

resolution

image size and, 26-27

Print Preview, 174

retouching

color adjustments with Adjustment
Layer, 54-55

color balance, 53

color calibration for monitors, 42-44

color-cast adjustments, 51

color enhancements, 53-54

color variations, 52-53

contrast adjustments, 48-51

cover up tools, 57-59

fine-tuning tools, 59

lighting adjustments, 47-48

red eye, 56-57

scanned images, 46

sharpening details, 59-61

softening harsh edges, 61-62

tools for, 13-14

RGB color, 102, 104

Ripple filter, 148

Rotate command, 8, 74

Rough Pastel filter, 147

Rulers, turning on/off, 7

Rusted Metal effect, 97, 162

S

Sandpaper effect, 162

Saturation/Hue, color enhancements, 53-54

Save As command, 170

Save As dialog box, 168-169

Save command, 168

Save for Web, 180-181

Save In menu, Windows, 169

saving images, 168-172

    destinations, 169-170

    file format options, 169

    file formats, changing, 170-172

    naming files, 168-169

    Save As command, 170

    Save command, 168

Scale command, 73

Scaled Print Size settings, Print Preview, 174

scanned images

    importing, 38

    retouching, 46

scanners

    connecting to, 2

    importing images from, 38

scatter option, Brush tool, 114

Scratch Disk, 18-19

scroll bars, Image Window, 16

selection border, 64-65

Selection Brush, 67

selection mode, Magnetic Lasso tool, 76

selection tools, 63-84

    adding to selections, 70-71

    complex selections, 75-79

copying and pasting, 72

cropping images, 64-66

flipping, 73

illustration of, 67

incorporating copies, 81-82

inverse selections, 83-84

irregular selections, 67-70

modifying selections, 79-81

moving, 74-75

pixel selection with, 13

rotating, 74

scaling, 73

simple selections, 66-67

subtracting from selections, 71-72

shadow effects, 96, 153-155

Shape tool, 123

shapes

    adding to layers, 123

    selecting irregular, 67-70

    selecting simple, 66-67

sharing images

    e-mailing, 177-178

    over Web, 179-182

    with Photo Gallery, 182-185

    slide shows, 178-179

Sharpen tool, 60-61

sharpening details, 59-61

Shield option, Crop tool, 65

Shortcuts bar

    illustration of, 4

    options of, 9

Similar command, 80

Simplify Layer, 124

size options
  brushes, 113
  canvases, 29-30
  files, 136
  Image Window, 7
  images, 24-25, 181, 184-185
  palettes, 10
  printed images, 173, 174
  resolution and, 26-27
  type, 88
Skew command, type, 93
slide shows, 178-179
Smooth command, 80-81
Smudge Stick filter, 146
Smudge tool
  blending paints, 116-117
  cleaning up blemishes, 57
softening harsh edges, 61-62
spacing options, Brush tool, 114
stacking order, layers, 129
Stagger option, wind filters, 150
start up, 2
Status bar, 6
Step Backward/Step Forward buttons,
  Shortcuts bar, 9
stock photographs, 122
Straighten and Crop Image command, 46
Style settings, 119, 155
styles
  categories of. See also layer styles
  combining with filters and effects, 162
  impressionist, 145-146
  surrealist, 146-147
Styles menu, 183

surrealist style, 146-147
Swatches palette, 104-106
  adding colors to, 106-107
  color library selection, 104-105
  loading paint colors to, 104

T

text. See type
Text Color box, Options bar, 90
text Warp, 91-93
textures, 162-165
Textures library, 160, 162
Texturizer filter, 147, 162-163
Thumbnail images, 127
thumbnail layer, 124
Thumbnail View icon, Filters palette, 145
thumbnails, of color swatches, 105
TIFF (.tif) file format, 172
Title bar, Image Window, 5
Tolerance settings, 79, 119
tonal range, 47, 51
Toolbox
  illustration of, 4
  selecting tools, 13-14
  setting tool options, 14-15
tools. See also by individual tool
  creation tools, 14
  miscellaneous tools, 14
  retouch tools, 13-14
  selection tools, 13
transform options, type, 93-94
  Perspective command, 94
  Skew command, 93

transparency, of images, 131-132

Tutorial option, Welcome Screen, 2-3

TWAIN interface, 39

type

    adding to layers, 124-125

    aligning, 89

    anti-aliasing, 88-89

    color, 90

    depth options, 95-96

    editing, 87

    entering, 86-87

    fill options, 97-100

    fonts, 88

    formatting, 87

    moving, 90

    orienting, 90

    resizing, 88

    transforming, 93-94

    Warp effect, 91-93

type layer, 87, 94-95

Type Mask tool, 98-100

Type tools

    adding type layer with, 124-125

    Horizontal, 86, 90

    Options bar, 88

    Vertical, 90

typeface, 88

U

Undo History palette, 10-12

Undo/Redo buttons, Quick Fix window, 46

Unsharp Mask filter, 59-60

V

vector art, 123

vector images, 23, 93

Vertical Type tool, 90

video cameras, 39-40

video stills, 39-40

View menu, 8

Vignette effect, 159

W

Warp effects, 91-93

    making waves, 91-93

    overview of, 91

    surrealist effect with, 146

water illusion, 148

Wave filter, 148

waves effects, typographic, 91-93

Web Photo Gallery, 182-185

    applying, 185

    options, 184-185

    setting up, 182-183

Web Photo Gallery dialog box, 183

Web Safe Colors, 105

Web, sharing images over, 179-182

Web sites

    digital color, 42

    getting help from Adobe web site, 20

Welcome Screen

    options, 2-3

    removing, 3

    retrieving, 8

Where menu, MacIntosh computers, 169

WIA (Windows Image Acquisition)
utility, 39

Width setting, Magnetic Lasso tool, 77

Wind filter, 149-150

Windows Image Acquisition (WIA)
utility, 39

Work Area

    illustration of, 4

    Menu Bar, 4

    Menu bar, 7-8

    Options bar, 4, 14-15

    organization of, 1

    overview of, 3-4

    palette management on, 10

    Palette Well, 4, 10-12

    Shortcuts bar, 4, 9

    Toolbox, 4, 13-15

Wow Plastic Layer Styles, 96

Z

Zoom tool, 15-16

INTERNATIONAL CONTACT INFORMATION

AUSTRALIA
McGraw-Hill Book Company Australia Pty. Ltd.
TEL +61-2-9900-1800
FAX +61-2-9878-8881
http://www.mcgraw-hill.com.au
books-it_sydney@mcgraw-hill.com

CANADA
McGraw-Hill Ryerson Ltd.
TEL +905-430-5000
FAX +905-430-5020
http://www.mcgraw-hill.ca

GREECE, MIDDLE EAST, & AFRICA
(Excluding South Africa)
McGraw-Hill Hellas
TEL +30-210-6560-990
TEL +30-210-6560-993
TEL +30-210-6560-994
FAX +30-210-6545-525

MEXICO (Also serving Latin America)
McGraw-Hill Interamericana Editores S.A. de C.V.
TEL +525-117-1583
FAX +525-117-1589
http://www.mcgraw-hill.com.mx
fernando_castellanos@mcgraw-hill.com

SINGAPORE (Serving Asia)
McGraw-Hill Book Company
TEL +65-863-1580
FAX +65-862-3354
http://www.mcgraw-hill.com.sg
mghasia@mcgraw-hill.com

SOUTH AFRICA
McGraw-Hill South Africa
TEL +27-11-622-7512
FAX +27-11-622-9045
robyn_swanepoel@mcgraw-hill.com

SPAIN
McGraw-Hill/Interamericana de España, S.A.U.
TEL +34-91-180-3000
FAX +34-91-372-8513
http://www.mcgraw-hill.es
professional@mcgraw-hill.es

UNITED KINGDOM, NORTHERN,
EASTERN, & CENTRAL EUROPE
McGraw-Hill Education Europe
TEL +44-1-628-502500
FAX +44-1-628-770224
http://www.mcgraw-hill.co.uk
computing_neurope@mcgraw-hill.com

ALL OTHER INQUIRIES Contact:
Osborne/McGraw-Hill
TEL +1-510-549-6600
FAX +1-510-883-7600
http://www.osborne.com
omg_international@mcgraw-hill.com

Finally!

because technology should
improve your life, not complicate it...

The No Nonsense approach
at a no frills price.